The Organ

A guide to its construction,
history, usage and music

David Baker

SHIRE PUBLICATIONS

Cover: *The organ of St Ignatius Loyola, New York City, USA. Built by N. P. Mander Ltd, 1992. The instrument is a large four-manual, with mechanical key and electric stop action. The specification owes much to French traditions, though the overall style is an eclectic one.*

ACKNOWLEDGEMENTS
I am very grateful to Tony Freeman-Cosh, of Picture Perfect Photography, Wymondham, Norfolk, who spent much time producing photographs of the outside and the inside of the organs of Wymondham Abbey.

Pictures are acknowledged as follows: drawings by Rachel Beckett, page 9; Bildarchiv Foto Marburg, Frankfurt, page 36 (top); Birmingham City Council, page 55; Richard Bower, pages 47 (bottom), 93 (bottom left); Rodney Briscoe, pages 69, 70, 72, 73, 75, 76, 77; *Cheshire Life* magazine, courtesy of Charles Legh, page 43; Church of Scotland, Department of Communication, page 54 (bottom); Peter Collins, Leicester, page 65 (top two); English Heritage, page 61; Goetze & Gwynn, pages 12 (bottom), 46, 53, 62 (top), 87, 92 (bottom), 93 (top; bottom right), 100 (bottom two); Harrison & Harrison, Durham, page 21; Ernest Hart, page 62 (bottom); J. W. Hinton, *Organ Construction*, 1910, pages 7, 8, 10 (bottom), 12 (top), 13, 15; Cox Knuf-Jongman at Frits Knuf BV Buren, page 20; Cadbury Lamb, page 45; Laurie Lambrecht, page 57; Lammermuir Pipe Organs, page 23; Landesinstitut für Pädagogik und Medien, Dudweiler, page 24; Daniel Malnati, Waltzing-Arlon, Belgium, pages 39 (right), 40; Noel Mander & Co, cover, pages 4, 25, 44, 48, 56, 64 (both), 65 (bottom), 92 (top), 94, 100 (top two and centre left), 109, 110, 118; National Gallery of Scotland (by gracious permission of Her Majesty The Queen), page 22; Picture Perfect, Wymondham, pages 5, 6 (bottom), 11 (both), 14, 16, 47 (top), 52 (top); Praetorius, *Syntagma Musicum II*, pages 6 (top), 27, 28, 30 (top), 31; Priory Records, pages 38, 58; Rijksdienst voor Monumentenzorg Zeist, Holland, page 33; Rushworth & Dreaper, page 107; Thomas-Photos, page 98; Thursford Collection, page 60; Kenneth Tickell & Co, pages 51, 97, 100 (centre right), 105; Ian Tracey, page 10 (top); J. W. Walker & Sons, pages 52 (bottom), 54 (top), 66; Joan Welsby, pages 88 (both), 91; Peter Williams, pages 29, 30 (bottom), 32 (both), 34, 35 (both), 36 (bottom), 37, 39 (left), 41, 42, 82, 83, 85. The musical examples on pages 74, 78, 79, 80, 81, 86, 89 and 90 are by Joan Welsby.

British Library Cataloguing in Publication Data:
Baker, David.
The organ: a guide to its construction, history, usage and music. – New ed.
1. Organ (Musical instrument) – History
I. Title
786.5'19
ISBN-10 0 7478 0560 1.

Published in 2013 by Shire Publications Ltd, Midland House, West Way, Botley, Oxford OX2 0PH. (Website: www.shirebooks.co.uk)
Copyright © 1991 and 2003 by David Baker. First published 1991; reprinted 1993. Second edition revised and expanded 2003; reprinted 2010, 2011 and 2013. ISBN 978 0 74780 560 1.
David Baker is hereby identified as the author of this work in accordance with Section 77 of the Copyright, Designs and Patents Act 1988.

Printed in China through Worldprint Ltd.

Contents

Preface to the revised second edition

The first edition of this book was in print for some twelve years. During that time a large number of new organs were built, and historic ones restored. In addition, some startling discoveries were made – in particular the remains of two pre-Reformation English organs, discussed in the text.

I have again taken the opportunity to update the text and make further necessary corrections and additions. The work is intended as a general introduction to the subject for all who wish to learn something about the instrument, though it is perhaps of most value to those who have little or no previous knowledge of the organ, its history, construction, usage and repertoire. For those wishing to find out more than this book can provide in its 120 pages, the 'further reading' section gives a wide range of useful titles, though not all are in print. I continue to hope that my book will guide and inform those who wish to learn more about this noblest of instruments.

DAVID BAKER
Mytholmroyd,
West Yorkshire,
2009

The organ of Magdalen College, Oxford. Built by N. P. Mander Ltd, 1986. The 1830s stone case at the front of the screen houses the Great organ, in the 'Chair' position, with a new wooden case containing the Swell and Pedal. Though the instrument has only two manual divisions, there are three manuals, with the third one being a 'coupling' keyboard playing Great and Swell together. The instrument has mechanical action throughout.

1
How an organ works

What is an organ? Sir Christopher Wren, architect of St Paul's Cathedral, London, described the instrument as a 'kist of whistles'. He was being uncomplimentary (he disagreed violently with the man who was building the organ for the cathedral), but his description was basically correct. The pipe organ is little more than a box of 'whistles' activated by one or more keyboards (similar to those found on pianos or harpsichords) and supplied with air from a bellows (like those used to help light a fire).

The pipes

A basic organ pipe, a *flue pipe*, makes its sound in much the same way as does the tin whistle or the recorder, in which the player's lungs are the bellows and provide the air. The air passes from his or her mouth (the equivalent of the organ's windchest) and into a ducted windway and against a hard edge, causing an oscillation. In the case of the organ flue pipe, the wind enters through the *foot* of the pipe. As the air is split within the organ pipe, it vibrates and creates sound. The sound is then magnified through the rest of the pipe. Putting fingers over the holes on the recorder makes the instrument (and the column of air within it) longer and so the sound is lower in pitch. Organ pipes are the same: the longer they are, the lower the note.

Reed pipes make sound in a different way. The principle is as before: air passes into the pipe through its base and a vibration is set up between the reed *tongue* (usually made of brass) and the *shallot*, fixed inside the foot or boot of the pipe. This causes the column of air inside the *resonator* (the equivalent of the flue in flue pipes) to vibrate and make a sound. Several instruments of the orchestra make their sound in the same way, for example the oboe or the bassoon. Indeed, some of the stops

The large organ of Wymondham Abbey, Norfolk. Originally built by James Davis in 1793, the instrument retains almost all of the Davis pipework and the original case – a combination of the classical four-tower, three-flat style, with Gothick decorations.

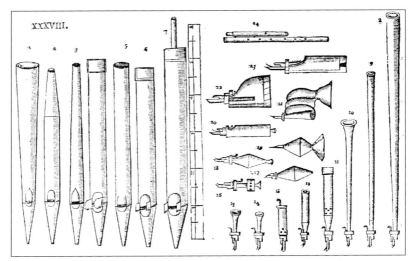

Various organ pipes, illustrated in Michael Praetorius, 'Syntagma Musicum II: De Organographia Parts I and II'. Note the different pipe lengths and shapes. Those on the right-hand side of the print are reed pipes.

The Great and Choir windchests of the Wymondham Abbey organ, seen from above. The smallest pipes are in the middle; the pieces of wood between the ranks and between the Great and Choir are 'passage boards' or walkways allowing the organ tuner easier access to the pipes. Note the wooden pipes, the stoppers and the different shapes of pipe tops, and the conveyancing tubes at the bottom of the picture.

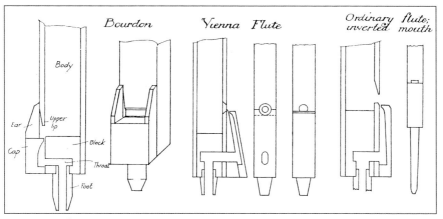

Various wooden pipes.

on an organ are called after instruments of the orchestra. In the nineteenth century, some organ builders used *free reeds*, where the shallot is replaced by a perforated oblong plate (usually made of thick brass) through which the tongue vibrates freely, hence the term. Free reeds could be made without resonators and led to the construction of the *harmonium*, discussed in chapter 2.

The length of a pipe affects the pitch of the note produced and in an organ of average size the pipes vary in length from a few inches to 16 feet (4.9 metres). In larger instruments the biggest pipes may be 32 feet (9.8 metres) or longer.

Reed pipes sound different from flue pipes, in the way that an orchestral flute sounds different from an oboe. The shape of the organ pipe itself can alter the quality or timbre of the sound produced. The basic sound that an organ makes comes from the principal pipes. These are flue pipes with a simple cylinder above the pipe mouth. They make hard bright notes. If a stopper is placed in the top of the pipe, a much softer, fluty sound is produced, and the sound is twice as deep in pitch as that of an open pipe because the column of air is twice as long.

There are many other shapes of organ pipe, each of which alters the sound in some way. Some pipes are conical; others are stopped but with an open chimney sticking out of the top of the stopper; some are square; some are triangular; others are twice the length that they need to be, but with a hole in the middle. Most organ pipes are made of metal – usually an alloy of some kind (zinc, tin and lead are metals commonly used, though zinc tends to be used only for larger pipes). Pipes are often also made of wood. Wooden pipes are frequently stopped and usually produce a mellower sound than metal ones. Very occasionally other materials have been used, for example bamboo.

Metal flue pipes are tuned by lengthening the pipe to lower or flatten the pitch and by shortening it to raise or sharpen the pitch. This is usually done by means of a tuning slide, a cylinder of metal which fits around the top of the pipe and which can be moved up or down to lengthen or shorten the pipe as required. In older organs, flue pipes were tuned by opening out the top of the pipe and broadening the diameter to sharpen the pitch or narrowing the pipe to flatten it. This was done

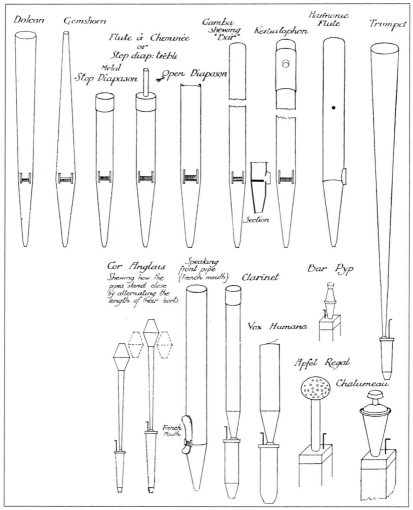

Various metal pipes.

by means of a tuning cone, a cone-shaped tool whose narrow end was inserted into the pipe to open it up and sharpen it or whose hollow broad end was put over the top of the pipe to narrow and flatten it. The tuning cone would be driven into the pipe using a hammer. This tended to damage the pipes over a period of time, hence the use of tuning slides. Some pipes, especially those in case-fronts, are tuned by peeling away a strip of metal at the top of the pipe and hence shortening or (if the

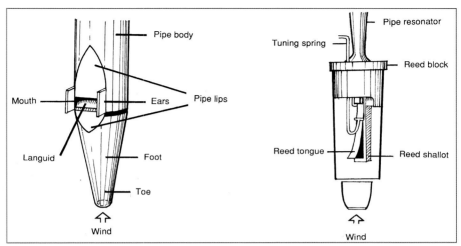

Above left: *A typical flue pipe. In flue pipes the wind enters through the toe and into the foot from the windchest on which the pipe is sitting. The toe fits into a hole in the windchest and the foot is usually supported upright by a wooden rack. The wind travels up through the foot to the mouth, where it is forced through a narrow passage between the languid, which blocks off all but the very front of the pipe, and the pipe mouth itself. This causes the column of air to vibrate and make a sound. The sound comes out through the mouth and, if the pipe is open at the top, through there as well. The languid may be nicked by the organ-pipe voicer in order to alter the way in which the pipe 'speaks'. The pipe body will vary in length depending upon the pitch of the note and whether it is an open or a stopped pipe, and its shape on the kind of register (principal, flute, and so on).*

Above right: *A typical reed pipe. Wind enters the pipe through the foot, as in a flue pipe. Inside the foot of the pipe is the reed shallot against which the reed tongue vibrates when the air enters. The reed tongue and shallot are mounted on the reed block, on which is also mounted the pipe resonator. The tuning spring is linked to the tongue and allows the organ tuner to alter the length of the reed tongue and so change its pitch. The length of the resonator will vary according to the pitch of the pipe and the type of register. Reed pipes are usually made of metal, though the resonators, especially in larger pipes, are also made of wood. Altering the length of the resonator also changes the pitch.*

metal is rolled back up) lengthening the pipe. Stopped flue pipes are tuned by adjusting the stopper up or down within the pipe. Reed pipes are tuned by adjusting the length of the reed in order to make it vibrate more rapidly (producing a higher note) or more slowly (producing a lower note) or by changing the length or shape of the resonator. The organ builder can alter the way in which the pipes speak (that is, sound) by varying the basic dimensions or scaling of the pipe or by altering the way in which it is voiced. For instance, nicks in the piece of metal against which the air is forced to pass in a flue pipe (the languid) can alter the quality of the sound and the speed at which it is produced. The timbre and volume can also be altered by the pressure of the air entering the pipe. The wind pressure is measured by the extent to which the air coming from the bellows can move a

The choir console of Liverpool Anglican Cathedral, 1960. Note the significant number of registration aids and the swell or crescendo pedals. It is possible to see why the French call toe pistons mushrooms!

water or similar gauge. On smaller or older instruments, pressure is typically 1.5 to 2.5 inches (3.8 to 6.4 cm). On larger organs, and especially those built in the latter part of the nineteenth and the first half of the twentieth century, wind pressures are often considerably higher. Two of the reed stops of the organ at Liverpool Anglican Cathedral are on 50 inches (127 cm) pressure.

The mechanism

So that the organ can make a sound, air has to reach the pipes. The bellows supply the air. Before the advent of electricity, organs had to be hand-blown. In some old country churches it is still possible to see the pumping lever that fills the bellows with air. Other ways of providing the wind included men standing on the bellows or in treadmills. It is thought that some ancient organs used water to provide air to the pipes (see chapter 2). More recently hydraulic and gas engines have been used to fill the bellows, though most organs are now supplied with air by an electric blower.

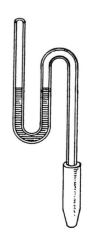

A wind gauge; the wind pressure is measured by the extent to which the pressure from the windchest moves the column of water in the gauge.

Above left: *The organ bellows and tracker action of the Wymondham Abbey organ.*
Above right: *The electric action of the Wymondham Abbey organ.*

From the bellows the air is supplied to the windchest by means of trunking. The windchest is a wooden box with holes on top into which the pipes fit. Pipes of the same type are grouped together in ranks. A *rank* denotes a grouping of pipes of the same type, construction and materials, with one pipe for every note on the keyboard. Sometimes the pipes are arranged in order of size, with the largest ones at the left-hand or bass end of the windchest. Often, however, the pipes are placed on the chest so that the largest pipes are either all in the middle or at either end. This prevents the big pipes from drawing the wind to one end of the chest. There are different types of windchest, but the one most commonly found uses *sliders* (see page 13).

The instrument is played from one or more keyboards. Those played by the hands are usually called manuals (*manus* is the Latin word for hand). The larger pipes are played from a special keyboard designed to be used by the organist's feet. The pedals normally control the bigger pipes.

The keyboards are linked to the windchest and hence the pipes by the action or key mechanism. Several different kinds of action exist. The oldest and most durable is known as *tracker* or *mechanical* action. Here, the keys are linked by a series of trackers (thin trace rods, usually made of wood) to pallets underneath the windchest. When a key is depressed, the pallet is activated and allows wind into the pipes immediately above it. Because the windchest is bigger than the keyboard and in many cases the pipes are not arranged in the same order as the keys, the tracker action incorporates a *roller board*, which ensures that the keys allow the correct

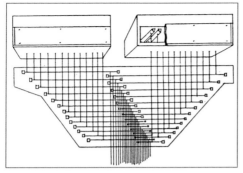

A roller board.

pipes to sound, even if they are not situated above that part of the keyboard to which they relate. The most extreme example of this matching is the bottom C sharp key, which on many organs will have its pipes at the top (right-hand) end of the windchest – as far away as they can be from the key.

Some organs have tubular-pneumatic, electro-pneumatic or electric action. In a *tubular-pneumatic* action the trackers are replaced by small tubes that link the keys to the pallet. When a key is depressed, air within the tube activates a pneumatic motor or valve, which then allows wind into the pipes above. In an *electro-pneumatic* action the tube is replaced by electric wiring. Depressing the key completes an electric circuit, which in turn activates the pneumatic motor. In an *electric* action the pallet is operated by a magnet (brought into use by completion of the electrical circuit as the key is depressed) instead of a pneumatic motor. Even when the key action is not tracker, the linkage from the swell pedal to the corresponding shutters

is often a mechanical one in order to ensure the best control over the crescendo and diminuendo. However, in the nineteenth and twentieth centuries a number of pneumatic and other actions were invented with the aim of allowing a similar fine dynamic gradation.

Chamber organ made by Goetze & Gwynn in 1998 for the Handel House Trust, which in 2001 opened a museum in the house where Handel lived for the last thirty-six years of his life, at 25 Brook Street, Westminster, London. The instrument lives at St George's, Hanover Square. It is based on the chamber organs of Richard Bridge and Thomas Parker. There is a 'shifting movement' pedal at the left of the base, which removes the metal ranks if drawn. The large pedal at the right allows the instrument to be blown by foot.

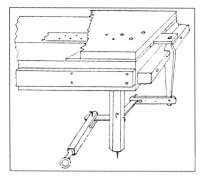

A simple mechanical stop action, linking the stopknob to the slider on the windchest.

There are other types of action and windchest, though the basic principles remain the same. Tracker action allows the player to be in close contact with the instrument and the pipes. A much more sensitive touch can be used with such an action and a good player can articulate the sound of the pipes by the way in which he or she depresses the key. Tubular-pneumatic and electric actions are less sensitive, since there is no real contact between the player's fingers and the pallets. However, in very large instruments, or in locations where there is a need to have the keyboards separated from the pipes, then tracker action is often not feasible. Wherever possible, most organ builders now prefer to build traditional mechanical actions.

The layout and tonal design

The variety of sound in an organ comes from ranks of pipes not only of different pitches but of different shapes and in different locations too. Before a pipe can sound, it has to be *voiced* by an expert member of the organ-building team. The 'voicer' adjusts every pipe in the rank to make sure that they all 'speak' or sound in the same way, evenly throughout the compass of the keyboard, and that they are balanced with the other ranks on the organ. Voicing is a very special skill, and needs to take into account the position of the organ and the acoustics of the building in which it is situated. The ranks of pipes can usually be played separately or in combination, except in the case of the higher-pitched ranks, which are often grouped together. Because these pipes are very small even in the lowest part of their compass, the ranks consist of the same size of pipe further up the scale so that they do not become too small to be made and to sound effectively. These groups of ranks are known as *mixture* stops.

The organist sits at a *console*, where there are the keyboards and the pedals. In most church organs, on either side of the console are the *stopknobs*, which control the ranks of pipes. There are other types of stop control such as small *stoptabs* placed above the top row of keys or even in between the manuals to facilitate rapid stop changes. If the organist sits down at the console, switches on the organ blower and then plays a chord on one of the manuals, nothing will happen unless one or more of the stops is pulled out. Originally, the stop mechanism caused wind to be shut off from certain ranks, hence the term, but nowadays the stop has to be in the 'on' position for the rank to sound. Beneath each rank or group of ranks of pipes on the windchest is a mechanism that stops wind from entering the pipes unless the player wishes the pipes to sound. In organs with tracker action, the mechanism is usually called a *slider*. In the 'on' position, the holes in the slider match with those in the windchest and allow the air through to the pipes; in the 'off' position, the slider holes do not match with those in the windchest and the air cannot enter the pipes.

There are other mechanisms for shutting off the wind supply, but the basic principle is the same as with the slider. Choosing the most appropriate combination of stops is part of the organist's art and is discussed in chapter 3.

The manuals and pedals each control different sets of ranks on one or more windchests. Large instruments can have as many as four or five manuals and over one hundred stops. Most instruments have two or three manuals and pedals and between twenty and forty stops. Some instruments – usually called *chamber organs* – have only one manual and no pedals.

The groups of pipe ranks controlled by each manual or the pedals are usually called *divisions*, though sometimes they are called 'organs', recalling the time when several different instruments were combined into one larger one. Each division has its own windchest and a different name. *Pedal* is an obvious one; the names of the other divisions require explanation, however. The *Great* division (or organ) is so called because it contains the main set of principal stops (usually called a chorus) and sounds grand and imposing. The *Swell* manual controls a division that is enclosed in a box with a set of shutters (usually looking like a Venetian blind) at the front. These shutters are operated by a *swell pedal* at the organist's feet. As they open, the sound gets louder or 'swells'. The *swell box* and its shutters enable the player to crescendo and diminuendo.

Most organs in Britain have Great, Swell and Pedal divisions. If there is a third manual it usually controls the *Choir* division. It was often thought that this term originated because the stops on this windchest were included in order to accompany choral music. However, the word 'choir' is a corruption of the word 'chair'. In older British and continental organs (as well as some more recent instruments) part of the instrument is placed in a separate section behind where

the player sits, hence the term *Chair* organ (the pipes are behind the organist's chair).

Some organs have a fourth manual, which controls a variety of stops. In many instruments this is called the *Solo* division, because the pipes are specially designed and voiced for playing melodic lines rather than full chords. The stops vary considerably both in timbre and power. Fourth (or fifth) manuals may also be labelled *Bombarde* or *Echo*. Bombarde divisions are made

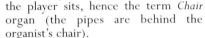

The swell shutters of the Wymondham Abbey organ. These shutters are horizontal and show the 'Venetian blind' origins of the device. Some shutters are placed vertically. The Wymondham Abbey organ shutters are controlled by a mechanical linkage to the swell pedal at the console.

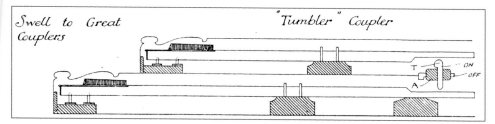

A simple coupler action to combine two manuals.

up of very powerful stops, as the name implies. An Echo section, on the other hand, consists of soft and delicate stops (usually in a swell box and perhaps placed some distance away from the main instrument), which can be used to echo the stops and sounds on the other, louder divisions.

In order to increase the power of the instrument, as well as to vary the sounds that can be produced, the manuals can usually be coupled together so that from one keyboard the pipes of two or more divisions can be made to sound at the same time. In mechanical-action instruments manuals are not all coupled together for long periods – especially if the touch is heavy – though larger tracker organs have electric or pneumatic coupling assistance mechanisms. In organs with other actions couplers can be freely provided and used. In some cases, for instance, it is possible to couple one manual to another at a different octave, or to couple a manual to itself at different octaves, with the option of having the original pitch silenced through the use of the 'unison off' device.

From time to time the organist will wish to change the *registration*, the combination of stops that have been drawn. It would soon become boring to the listener if the same sound came out of the instrument all the time. Stops can be changed by hand, and with older instruments that is the only option. On the European mainland it has often been the practice to employ an assistant to change the stops for the organist, it being difficult for the player to pull out or push in the drawstops and play the music at the same time. In most modern instruments, however, registration aids are provided. These may be foot pedals or pistons that push out combinations of stops when depressed. On some instruments there are also thumb pistons – little buttons between the manuals which bring out different combinations of stops when pushed in. Registration aids are most common on organs with pneumatic, electric or electro-pneumatic action.

The physical layout of the organ varies considerably from location to location, country to country and era to era. Mechanical-action organs must be in one place and follow a simple and logical layout if they are to function effectively and with a light keyboard touch. Other actions allow pipes to be placed in different locations, and it is not unknown for divisions to be placed in completely separate parts of a building. In some large churches, for instance, the main organ is too far away from the congregation to be heard effectively and so a separate *nave section* is built in order to lead hymn singing. This has its own wind supply and is connected to the

The organ console of Wymondham Abbey, a large three-manual organ by James Davis, 1793, rebuilt by Hill, Norman & Beard in 1954 and 1973. The manuals are (from the top): Swell, Great and Choir. The Great and Choir stops are on the right-hand jamb; the Swell and Pedal on the left. The organ has a typical number of registration aids. Below the lowest (Choir) manual at the extreme left and right of the keyboard are the general cancel piston, which takes all the stops off, and the piston setter switch, which allows the organist to alter the combinations brought out by the different pistons, when activated. Note the two 'reversible' toe pistons, to the right of the Swell pedal above the foot pedals, which provide a toggle control to the 16 and 32 foot Pedal reeds.

main instrument through an electric action.

Organs sound best when the pipes are enclosed at the back, sides and sometimes even the top by a case, usually made of wood. This focuses the sound and projects it into the building. An open location also ensures that the organ can easily be heard without the air being forced through the pipes. Unfortunately many organs, and especially those in churches, have been built without effective casing, or even with no casing at all, and in poor, cramped locations.

The specification

The specification of an organ consists of a list of the stops, couplers and registration aids that the instrument possesses. The specification cannot tell how an instrument sounds, but it does give some indication of the range and nature of the various stops and the tone colours that they produce.

The large pipe organ of Wymondham Abbey, Norfolk, is well known for its fine sound and provides a typical example. The organ has three manuals and a Pedal division. Each division has a chorus of principal stops as its foundation.

The term *Open Diapason* is used in English organs to denote the basic principal

The specification of the organ of Wymondham Abbey, Norfolk.

GREAT ORGAN		SWELL ORGAN	
Double Stopped Diapason	16+	Open Diapason	8
Open Diapason	8	Hohlflute	8
Stopped Diapason	8	Salicional	8
Dulciana	8	Voix Celeste (TC)	8
Principal	4	Principal	4
Block Flute	4	Fifteenth	2
Twelfth	2⅔	Cornet	12-15-17 III
Fifteenth	2	Mixture	19-22 II
Seventeenth	1⅗	Contra Hautboy	16
Mixture	19-22 II	Trumpet	8
Sharp Mixture	22-26-29 III	Basset Horn	8
Trumpet	8	Clarion	4
Clarion	4	Tremulant	
Swell to Great		Swell Octave	
		Swell Suboctave	
		Swell Unison Off	

CHOIR ORGAN		PEDAL ORGAN	
Chimney Flute	8	Open Wood Bass	16
Viola da Gamba	8	Contra Gamba	16
Principal	4	Bourdon	16+
Stopped Flute	4	Octave	8+
Flageolet	2	Gamba	8+
Larigot	1⅓	Gedackt	8+
Cymbel	29-33-36 III	Fifteenth	4+
Trumpet	8*	Mixture	19-22 II
Clarion	4*	Sackbut	32
Swell to Choir		Ophicleide	16
		Clarion	8*
		Shawm	4
		Swell to Pedal	
		Great to Pedal	
		Choir to Pedal	

6 adjustable thumb pistons to each manual.
6 adjustable toe pistons to Great/Pedal and Swell.
reversible thumb pistons to manual to Pedal couplers, Swell to Great coupler.
reversible toe pistons to Swell to Great and Great to Pedal couplers, 16 foot and 32 foot reed
   stops.
reversible thumb piston for Swell tremulant.

* Denotes borrowed from Great Organ.
+ Denotes extended rank.

---

stop in the organ. The word 'Diapason' comes from the Greek and approximates to the phrase 'of full compass'. The figures relate to the length, in feet, of the longest pipe of each rank. Thus the 4 foot Principal plays an octave higher than the 8 foot Diapason, and the Fifteenth two octaves higher. The Fifteenth is so called because it plays fifteen white notes (naturals) higher than the 8 foot stop; the Twelfth is twelve notes higher and the Seventeenth seventeen notes higher. The Twelfth and Seventeenth, and any other ranks whose longest pipe measurement includes a fraction (for example 1⅓, 1⅗, 2⅔), sound thirds and fifths away from the fundamental sound rather than octaves. They are called *mutation stops* because they change the basic pitch. For example, if the Twelfth stop is drawn on its own and the bottom C key is depressed, the note G $1\frac{1}{2}$ octaves above is sounded.

As already noted, the very high-pitched ranks are grouped together as mixtures. The Roman numerals denote the number of ranks that are controlled by one stop and the figures show how far above the fundamental 8 foot pitch the pipes sound. Thus $19 = 19$ notes, $22 = 22$ notes, and so on. The III rank mixture is called 'sharp' because of the bright edgy tone that its high ranks add to the Great organ chorus. The higher-pitched stops are not normally played on their own, but in combination with 8, 4 and 2 foot pitch stops.

Each division has other kinds of ranks apart from the principals. The Great organ, for instance, has three flute stops, the Double Stopped Diapason, the Stopped Diapason and the Block Flute. The first two, as their names imply, are made up of stopped pipes. The Block Flute is an open rank, but with cone-shaped pipes. The division is completed by two reed stops, the Trumpet and the Clarion. These ranks can be played from both the Great and the Choir manuals. If played from the Choir keyboard, they can be accompanied on the Great manual, or *vice versa*. The Trumpet and Clarion are very loud stops, best used for solo purposes, for the pipes are mounted horizontally high up inside the case. Ranks located in this position are described as being *en chamade*, the French phrase for sounding a battle fanfare. At the other extreme is the Dulciana, probably the quietest rank on the organ. It has very small-scale pipes and is voiced as a very soft principal stop.

The pipes of the Pedal division are twice the size of those on the manuals, for the most part; the 16 foot stops are the equivalent of the 8 foot stops on the manuals, for example. The higher-pitched Pedal stops can be used to play solos while the manuals provide the accompaniment. The Shawm (named after the predecessor of the orchestral oboe) is the best stop to use for this purpose. Its pungent reedy tone can be heard clearly above the accompaniment, played on the manuals. The Sackbut (the name for the medieval trombone) is the largest and one of the loudest stops on the organ. It adds a deep growling bass to the louder combinations on the manual divisions.

The 16 foot Pedal Bourdon is one of the commonest organ stops and provides a gentle bass sound. The word comes from the French *bourdonner*, 'to buzz'. The word 'Gamba' is short for 'viola da gamba'; the organ stop is meant to imitate the instrument from which it takes its name. It has a firm cello-like sound. The Ophicleide is another powerful reed stop and sounds like the manual Trumpet ranks, except an octave lower. Like those of many of the stops on an organ, the name comes from an old orchestral instrument, in this case the predecessor of the bassoon. This use of the names of early instruments to describe organ stops shows how the main phase of organ development took place in the fifteenth, sixteenth and seventeenth centuries, when such orchestral instruments were prevalent and organ builders attempted to imitate them in their organs.

On organs with pneumatic, electric or electro-pneumatic actions, and exceptionally on mechanical-action instruments, it is possible to use the same set of pipes to make up different stops. As already noted, the Great Trumpet and Clarion can also be played from the Choir manual and (in the case of the Trumpet) the pedals because electric actions from the three divisions can activate these pipes. This technique of 'borrowing' stops or pipes is often applied in modern organs. At Wymondham Abbey, for instance, the lower part of the Great Double Stopped Diapason provides the bass pipes for the Pedal Bourdon, while the Flute, the Gamba and the Fifteenth all share pipes with their 16 or 8 foot equivalent. Extending ranks in this way so that they form two or more stops of the same type at different pitches saves metal or wood, space and money. The principle of *extension* has been used throughout some organs, though in such cases the organ tone may sound thinner than it would if at least all the main ranks were independent of each other. Where space and funds are scarce, however, extension of ranks can help to provide a bigger Pedal division than would otherwise be the case.

The Swell stops can sound loud or soft because of their enclosure in the swell box. The Salicional (from the latin *salix*, 'willow reed') and Voix Celeste (French for 'celestial voice') are string stops. The pipes are small and narrow in scale and are voiced in such a way as to produce a sound similar to stringed instruments such as the violin and viola. The two ranks are slightly out of tune with each other in order to produce a beating effect similar to the vibrato on a violin. The Gamba stops on the Choir and Pedal divisions are also string stops. The Hohlflute is made of wood and has a hollow sound (the word *hohl* is German for 'hollow'). There are also principal stops on the Swell similar to those on the Great, including two mixtures. The Swell III rank mixture is labelled Cornet because the Seventeenth rank in its composition gives a brassy edge to the sound. The Swell division also contains four reed stops, all with names of orchestral instruments. When played together with the mixtures they produce a bright fiery sound. This is called the *Full Swell* effect. The Basset Horn is best used as a solo stop.

The Choir division is the smallest part of the organ. It has one Principal stop as the basis of the chorus and three flute stops. The 8 foot flute is made up of stopped metal pipes with little open chimneys in the tops of the stoppers. The 4 foot flute is made of stopped wooden pipes and the 2 foot Flageolet is made of open metal pipes. The Larigot is similarly constructed, being a high-pitched open flute stop. The Viola da Gamba is a string stop. The Cymbal is made of very small principal pipes and makes a bright tinkling sound.

All the stops are of full compass (that is, they operate throughout the keyboard or pedalboard) with the exception of the Voix Celeste, which stops at Tenor C (the C note that would be the lowest of the tenor voice's range). The specification shows which of the manuals can be coupled to each other and to the pedals. The Swell manual can be coupled to itself at the octave and sub-octave pitches, with the option of switching off the unison pitch at the same time. The Tremulant acts on the supply of wind to the Swell division and disturbs the flow so that the pipes sound as if they have a vibrato like the human voice or a stringed instrument. This device normally affects only the softer stops, and especially those that are most likely to be used for a solo.

The stop names do not say what materials the pipes are made of, with the exception of the large Open Wood stop on the Pedal division. In some organs more of the stop names include reference to their wood or metal construction.

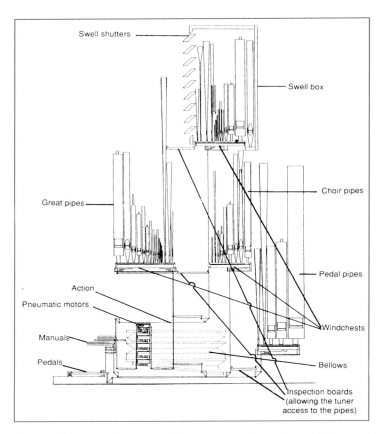

General section of an organ, showing sound boards and stops in profile, and the 'pneumatic key' (Barker lever). Originally published in Hopkins and Rimbault, 'The Organ: Its History and Construction', 1877.

The Wymondham Abbey organ uses a combination of tracker action (the original mechanism of 1793), electro-pneumatic and electric actions (installed in 1954). Because the sliders are activated by electro-pneumatic action, it is possible to provide a number of *registration aids*. Thus there are six *thumb pistons* for each manual division and pedal, duplicated by *toe pistons* in the case of the Swell and Great divisions. When pressed, these pistons bring out various *stop combinations*, as determined by the organist. The pistons can be altered at will. Other pistons control particular stops or couplers, as noted on the specification. These pistons are all *reversible*. In other words, if the stop or coupler is not in use when the piston is pressed, it is activated. If it is in use, then pressing the piston withdraws the stop or coupler. The organ case has four *towers* and three *flats* of pipes. A flat is just that: a straight row of pipes. A tower groups the pipes in a semi-circle curving out from the case. Nineteenth and early twentieth-century organs often

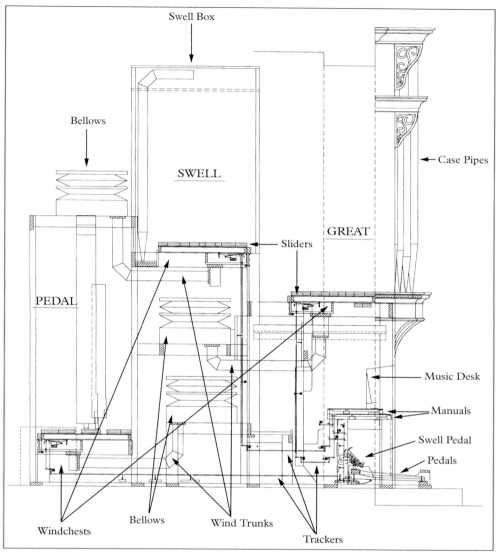

Cross-section of a design drawing from a modern two-manual and pedal mechanical-action organ built by Harrison & Harrison, Durham, for Emmanuel Church, Chestertown, Maryland, USA. The wind pressures are 2¾ inches for the manuals and 3 inches for the pedal.

did not have real cases, but only a rack of pipes at the front of the instrument to hide the inner pipes and mechanism. This is not the situation at Wymondham Abbey, where the organ case is an imposing creation, complete with pinnacles and cherubs!

A fifteenth-century positive organ from a painting of 1476 by Hugo van der Goes in the National Gallery of Scotland. Note the modern keyboard, the chromatic arrangement (large to small from bass to treble) of the pipes, and the large drone or bass pipes at the left-hand side of the case. The second angel at the back of the case is presumably blowing the organ!

2

History and types

Early history

According to legend, the organ developed from the *syrinx* or Pan-pipes. The *syrinx* was essentially a rank of pipes of different lengths, each pipe playing one note when blown. The first record of such ranks of pipes being operated mechanically dates from *c.*250 BC, when a Greek engineer named Ktesibios is reputed to have invented the *hydraulos* (Latin, *hydraulus*). The *hydraulos* consisted of a simple rank of pipes activated from a crude keyboard and a wind supply controlled by water pressure. The instrument was often used at festivals to accompany celebrations.

Parts of a small Roman organ, dated to AD 228 and found at Aquincum, Hungary, have survived. The instrument appears to have had four ranks of pipes, one open and three stopped, of thirteen notes each, mounted on a wooden windchest with slides underneath to allow wind into the pipes. Nothing is known about how air was fed into the pipes of the Aquincum organ nor about the way in which the ranks were used.

However, it is known that by AD *c.*120 organs were being constructed with simple bellows to supply the wind. These instruments consisted of at most a few ranks and a series of sliders, which were pushed in and out to control the pipes. In early medieval instruments, the sliders were connected to large keys that were pushed by the hand or beaten with the fist. The organist was known as the *pulsator organorum* (beater of the organs).

Organs continued to be built after the fall of the Western Roman Empire. In AD 757 the Byzantine emperor is said to have presented an organ to King Pepin of France and a similar instrument is reputed to have been given to Charlemagne in 812. It is unlikely that the instruments of the Eastern Roman Empire were used in

A modern recreation of a positive organ, by Lammermuir Pipe Organs, after a painting by Jan Van Eyck. Note the 'wedge' bellows at the rear of the organ.

Hydraulus and cornu players; from a Roman mosaic of AD 230–40 at Nennig bei Trier, Germany.

churches; the Orthodox Church forbade use of the instrument. The organ was a secular instrument, as it had been in the earlier days of the Roman Empire, built to accompany a wide range of secular activities such as festivals, wedding feasts and gladiatorial contests.

Organs began to appear in churches from the tenth century onwards. It is not clear why this happened; perhaps the instrument's relative loudness or its association with public festivities made it seem appropriate to install organs in ecclesiastical buildings in order to enhance the services. Bishop Aldhelm wrote of the 'mighty voice' of the English organ in the seventh century AD. This power made the organ an attractive instrument for public gatherings, whether sacred or secular. The Benedictine order, for example, allowed the ringing of bells in church on festive occasions, and the use of an organ at high points in festal services would also

The organ in Holywell Music Room, Oxford, built in 1790 by Donaldson of Newcastle upon Tyne and restored by N. P. Mander Ltd in 1985. The instrument has no pedals, but a 'long compass' Great manual starting four notes below the modern manual compass; the Swell manual, on the other hand, has a 'short compass'. There is a shifting movement to silence the louder stops of the Great manual, when drawn.

have enriched the worship considerably. The Benedictine order had a strong interest in music and several of its members were leading writers on the subject. It was in their churches and monasteries that organs first began to appear. In AD c.990 an organ was built for Winchester Cathedral (a Benedictine church) that was said to consist of four hundred pipes and twenty-six bellows. The instrument required two organists playing separate 'slider' keyboards of twenty keys each. It has been suggested that organs such as that at Winchester were used to call worshippers to church because they could be heard from some distance away, in the same way that bells do nowadays.

Little is known about the exact size, nature or location of the medieval pipe organ and one can only conjecture as to the instrument's purpose. It would seem from surviving accounts of church services that the organ was used at the major festivals of the Christian year and may have accompanied the singing of the choir or provided interludes in the plainsong. Early instruments were placed near the doors of churches, perhaps because they were used for fanfares on great occasions; later medieval organs seem to have been located near to the singers' stalls. The west end of the church did not become a standard location until the seventeenth century.

The organ keyboard grew more sophisticated as organ building became more widespread. A medieval composition for the organ in the Robertsbridge Codex (c.1325) requires a keyboard with a middle octave similar to that found on a modern instrument. The separation of ranks into stops was possible as a result of the invention of the windchest in the fourteenth century. Once wind could easily be admitted into separate channels, one each for all the pipes relating to every single note on the keyboard, then it was possible to introduce sliders into the top of the windchest placed at 90 degrees to those channels in order to stop off selected ranks when required.

Until then, most organs consisted of only one manual of limited compass and one large mixture stop, including 8 foot and possibly also lower ranks. Gradually the compass of the manual increased and stop controls were introduced in order to allow ranks to be used separately from each other. Large church organs consisted mainly of multi-rank mixtures, with only a small number of 16, 8 and possibly 4 foot ranks controlled by stops. Variety was obtained by adding more manuals as much as by separating ranks on the same windchest. The organ built for Halberstadt Cathedral, Germany, in 1361, for example, had four keyboards, one being a series of levers activated by the knee, another a pedalboard played by the feet. The pipework of an organ such as that at Halberstadt would probably all have been open and made of metal.

It is not known when pedals first appeared. The first pedals may have been levers activated by the organist's knees; they may not have controlled a windchest or pipes but merely pulled down the lower manual keys. Later medieval organs contained a small number of low-pitched stopped pipes placed in a separate case; such pipes may have been activated by pedals, thus providing a bass to the higher-pitched pipes played from the manual keyboards.

At the same time as large church organs such as that at Halberstadt were being built, smaller 'positive' and 'portative' organs were being developed. Portative organs, as the name implies, were carried by the player, who pumped the bellows with one hand while playing a small keyboard with the other. Portative organs typically consisted of two or three short-compass ranks of open metal pipes.

The positive organ, on the other hand, was normally placed on the floor of the church (as opposed to on a chancel screen or gallery). The bellows were activated by a second person, thus allowing the organist to use both hands to play the keyboard. Like the portative, the positive organ would have only a few ranks, but the compass would be fuller, and stopped bass pipes similar to those in larger organs also seem to have been included. Two positive organs built in the fourteenth century survive. The National Historical Museum in Stockholm houses the case of an organ built c.1390 and consisting of up to six ranks, played from a single manual and pedals. An organ reputed to be of similar age still survives in playable condition

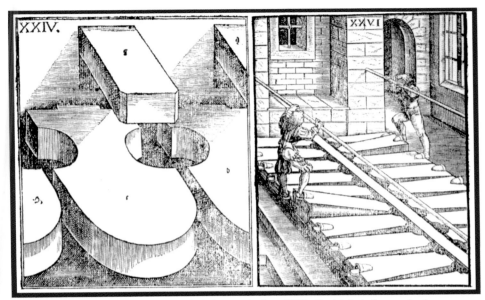

Manual keys of the Halberstadt Cathedral organ, built in 1361. (Right) Its bellows and calcants (bellows-men). Illustrated in Michael Praetorius, 'Syntagma Musicum II: De Organographia Parts I and II'.

at the Church of Nôtre Dame de Valère in Sion, Switzerland, though the organ has been subsequently altered so much that it is impossible to tell which parts date from the fourteenth century and how the pipes originally sounded.

By *c.*1450 reed stops began to appear. A small portable organ known as the *regal* also dates from this time. The regal consisted of a keyboard that let wind into small reed pipes, often made of wood, blown by hand-operated bellows. The reed inside the pipe determined the pitch and not the pipe length, which altered only the timbre. As a result the instrument took up little space. Very small regal organs were built so that they could be folded into the shape of a Bible. Regal pipes were increasingly incorporated into larger pipe organs. It is not known why the regal organ was so called. It is unlikely that it had any royal connection but the name may be a corruption of the Latin *regula*, a reference to the instrument's regulating the pitch of the singers whom it would be used to accompany.

A treatise on instrument construction written by Henri Arnaut in the mid fifteenth century refers to the making of different kinds of reed pipe and gives details of organs then extant. In particular, he talks about the construction of chair organs or back positives. Similar in design to earlier positive organs, these organs would be placed behind the organist's back or chair so that he could easily turn to play the instrument as a contrast from the large organ. The chair or back positive was soon made playable from a keyboard situated above or below those that activated the main organ, and to which the chair keyboard could be coupled. In older instruments, it is thought that while the keyboards were located together they were not necessarily aligned in such a way that they could be played together.

An old positive, illustrated in Michael Praetorius, 'Syntagma Musicum II: De Organographia Parts I and II'. Note the hand-operated bellows at the back of the instrument and the size of the pipes. The three small tabs at the side of the keyboard would have activated the sliders.

They may have continued to be regarded as separate instruments under the control of one person; some may have used different pitches for each manual depending upon the designated purpose (for example, to accompany singers).

By the beginning of the sixteenth century organ builders were becoming increasingly inventive in their organ-pipe manufacture, no doubt because their clients were becoming more demanding. In continental Europe organs were seen as a symbol of civic wealth, and towns and cities vied with each other over the size and splendour of the instruments in their churches. Many early contracts for organs specify that the instrument has to be bigger and better than other organs in the area. Keen to obtain lucrative contracts, organ builders promised larger and more powerful instruments with a greater variety of sounds than before. New kinds of pipe were introduced in order to increase the range of tone colours available to the organist. Reed stops that imitated other instruments – Cornet, Trumpet, Crumhorn, Sackbut – proved especially popular. Mutation stops such as the Nazard, Tierce and Larigot, all designed to provide additional colour to solo stop combinations, also appeared. The Tremulant was invented; organs even acquired moving statuary and other special effects such as the Cymbelstern, a rotating star with a bell on the end of each point that jingled when the star moved.

In 1511 Arnolt Schlick, a Bohemian, produced the first published book on the organ, his *Mirror of Organ-builders and Organists* (*Spiegel der Orgelmacher und Organisten*). He writes of organs that have a number of separate registers – principals, flutes, reeds, open and stopped pipes made of metal and of wood and of different shapes. The mechanism was little different from the modern tracker action and slider windchest. Schlick regarded the Pedal division as an extension of the main manual; indeed, in some organs the Pedal keyboard still activated stops placed on the windchest of the main division. However, it is clear from the music that Schlick himself wrote for the organ that the pedals would be expected to provide a full bass line to other parts played on the manual keyboards and a solo line accompanied by stops on the manuals, and to be capable of activating two, three and even four notes at the same time. This suggested that organists, at least in Germany, had to be capable of playing difficult pedal parts. Schlick also described the way in which organs were used in the church service. The instrument was to be used for the accompaniment of singers, the giving of notes to the priest intoning the service and the provision of musical interludes.

As the number of separable ranks on an organ increased, organists experimented with different ways of combining the stops to provide a wide variety of sounds. Chapter 3 discusses stop registration in detail. Surviving records of old organs and the way in which they were played show that only a small number of ranks would

The swallows' nest organ at the church of Nôtre Dame de Valère, Sion, Switzerland, c.1370. The pedal pipes were added in 1718 and the organ was restored in 1954. The keyboard is not original.

Positive and regal, illustrated in Michael Praetorius, 'Syntagma Musicum II: De Organographia Parts I and II'. Note the bellows and tuning implements. The 'pipes' of the regal can be seen immediately behind the keys. The instrument's size made it easily portable.

be combined at any one time. The amount of wind available to the organist on a hand-blown instrument would be limited. Only when mechanical blowing was introduced in the nineteenth century was it possible to combine a large number of stops together in the knowledge that there would be sufficient wind to enable all the ranks to sound properly. Organists in the sixteenth, seventeenth and eighteenth centuries concentrated on variety and subtlety in their stop registrations. Stop combinations on different divisions could also be contrasted with each other, while the Pedal division would include solo as well as chorus stops. The variety of sounds available to organists stimulated the composition of sets of variations on hymn tunes and plainchants, and in many of the north German and Dutch Protestant churches weekday organ recitals were regularly held from the sixteenth century onwards.

By the sixteenth century, then, all the basic elements of the pipe organ were well established. While organ builders across Europe interchanged ideas and built instruments in each other's countries (as, for example, Flemish builders in England), national styles of construction, layout and specification gradually emerged.

Germany, Holland, Scandinavia: the Werkprinzip organ

By the end of the sixteenth century organs in Germany, Holland and Denmark were often

Maria Langegg, Austria. The organ has the characteristic division of the main organ case, with the Rückpositiv in between, on the gallery edge.

Three-manual and pedal organ, illustrated in Michael Praetorius, 'Syntagma Musicum II: De Organographia Parts I and II'. Note the Rückpositiv organ behind the console, the Pedal towers at either side of the console and the main part of the instrument.

very grand instruments. Three- and four-manual organs became increasingly common. The arrangement of the stops and the divisions was normally determined by the *Werkprinzip* (a modern German word meaning literally 'work-principle', but perhaps more meaningfully translated as 'division system').

The *Werkprinzip* organ developed from the simple chorus or *Blockwerk* organs of the late medieval period. As more chorus divisions were added, and as an increasing number of ranks were separated from the 'block', each division acquired a particular character and position within the instrument. Thus the *Hauptwerk* (main division) had the largest chorus, based on an 8 foot or a 16 foot principal stop and placed in the centre of the instrument. The *Rückpositiv* (back positive) was placed behind the player's seat at the front of the gallery and was based on a 4 foot or possibly an 8 foot principal stop. The Rückpositiv would contain higher-pitched stops and in general have a sharper sound, partly because of the kind of ranks it contained and partly because of its position in relation to the rest of the instrument. The Pedal division would normally be divided between two large towers on either side of the Hauptwerk. Occasionally some or all of the ranks might be placed in or behind the main division.

Larger Werkprinzip organs contained other divisions. The *Oberwerk* (literally 'upperwork') was placed above the Hauptwerk. The *Brüstwerk* ('chestwork') was situated immediately above the console, almost facing the player's chest, hence the name. This division was often the smallest in size, typically being based on a 2 foot principal and containing delicately voiced stops.

The large Werkprinzip organs of Germany, Holland and Denmark represent a peak in organ building, which has rarely, if ever, been surpassed. Two of the finest organs of this kind are those of St Laurents, Alkmaar, and St Bavo, Haarlem, both in Holland.

The Alkmaar organ was rebuilt by F. C. Schnitger, a member of a famous family of seventeenth- and eighteenth-century organ builders, in 1723–6. The organ of

St Bavo was built in 1735–8 by Christiaan Müller. Both instruments are situated at the west end of large resonant churches. Each has three manuals (of which one controls a Rückpositiv) and a Pedal. The two organs have a wealth of principal ranks, complete with several mixtures, many different solo stops (both flue and reed) and a number of mutation ranks, which can be used both in the chorus combinations and to provide solo tone colours. The Alkmaar organ has brilliant mixtures as the main characteristic of its sound. At St Bavo the power comes more from the full-scaled principal ranks, some of which have two sets of pipes. Both instruments include narrow (male or Principal) and wide-scaled (female or Flute) stops on each manual. The cases of these

Above: *St Cosmo's, Stade, Germany. Three-manual organ by Arp Schnitger, 1675, in the classic Werkprinzip arrangement. The organ uses much material from an earlier instrument, a frequent occurrence with Schnitger organs.*

St Laurents, Alkmaar, Holland. Small organ in the choir, c.1511. Note the ornate late-Gothic case, with the tower decorations and the folding wing doors, used to protect the organ pipes from dust or sunlight when not in use.

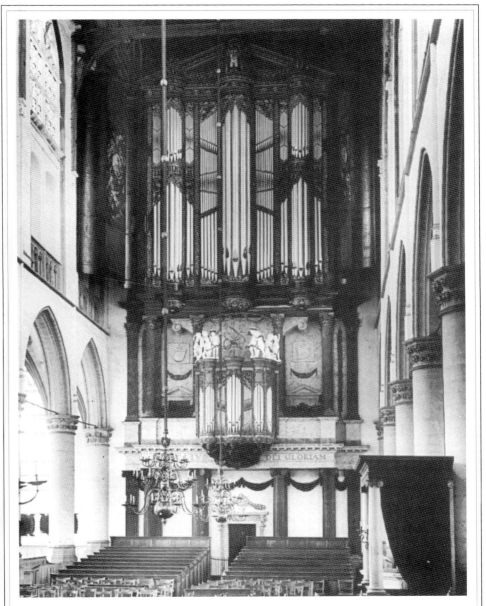

The organ of St Laurents, Alkmaar, Holland, 1638–45, rebuilt by F. C. Schnitger, 1723–6.

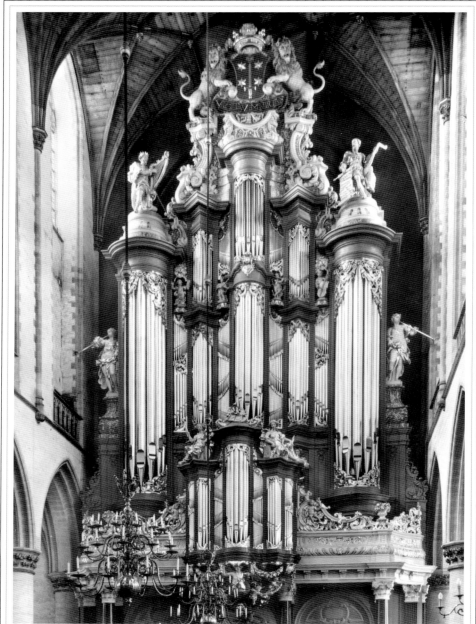

The organ of St Bavo, Haarlem, Holland, built in 1735-8 by Christiaan Müller. All the pipes are of metal.

organs are as grand as the instruments that they contain. The St Bavo case has lions, harpists and a range of classical statues on the tops and sides of the casework.

The Werkprinzip organ was found throughout Germany, Austria, Holland, Scandinavia and Poland. There were variations in design and layout according to region or builder, though the basic principle of a series of divisions, each with its own particular position within the instrument, lasted well into the nineteenth century in all these places. Such differences as there were related to the choice of divisions, the preference for 8 foot solo stops as opposed to mutation ranks, the style and composition (that is, the particular pitch and arrangement of the ranks) of the mixtures, or the size and specification of the Pedal division.

Thus, for example, in many later-eighteenth-century continental organs the Rückpositiv division was omitted in favour of a second or third manual division either above or below the Hauptwerk. Some builders used lower-pitched mixtures and 8 and 4 foot solo flues and reeds (as opposed to the higher-pitched mixture and solo stops of the Schnitger organ). One of the most famous Germanic organ-building families of this period, the Silbermanns, adopted this approach. The organ of Freiberg Cathedral, Saxony, is perhaps the best known example of their work, being built by Gottfried Silbermann

Above: *The organ of the Benedictine abbey of Weingarten, Germany, built in 1737–50 by Joseph Gabler. Note the twin Rückpositiv cases.*

Left: *Console of the organ in Weingarten Abbey. The organist faces away from the main pipework and is situated in between the two Rückpositiv cases.*

Ebermunster, Alsace, France. An organ built in the French style by A. and J. A. Silbermann, 1728–32. Note the shallowness of the main case and the organ illustration on the ceiling above.

between 1710 and 1714. A very different instrument, but one still part of the Werkprinzip tradition, is the organ of the Benedictine abbey of Weingarten, Bavaria. Much depended on the type of location, the attitude of the builder and designer and the kind of music that was to be played on the instrument.

The classical organ of France

French organs developed differently from the sixteenth century onwards. While the two main divisions, *Grande Orgue* and *Positif*, were similar to the Germanic Hauptwerk and Rückpositiv in location and design, the instruments built in France were very different in voicing and approach. For example, the Pedal division was much smaller than in most German and Dutch instruments, only having two or three stops of (usually) 8 foot or 4 foot pitch. These stops were included primarily so that the organist could play the melody with his feet while the manual parts provided an accompaniment. German organs could also do this, though the Pedal divisions on these also provided both a bass to the manual divisions and often an equal chorus to those of the other parts of the instrument.

The third and fourth manuals in French organs were usually an *Echo* organ, containing a full set of stops, but only for the upper part of the instrument's compass, and of softer voicing, and a *Récit* division, also of short compass, and with only one or two stops — usually a Cornet and perhaps a reed rank. Larger French organs of the eighteenth century also occasionally had Bombarde divisions containing loud reed stops that could be coupled either to the main manual or to the pedals.

By the middle of the seventeenth century French organs were designed according to certain basic principles, which were evident in almost all of the instruments constructed until the French Revolution put an end to organ building on any scale from 1790 until the 1840s. The principal choruses of the Grande Orgue and the Positif were based on a gently voiced stop, the Montre, so called because the bass pipes were shown in the case (*montrer* means 'to show'). The basic

The organ of Bordeaux Cathedral, France, built in 1748 by Bédos.

mixtures were called *Fourniture* because they 'furnished' the sound of the chorus, while the higher-pitched ones were called *Cymbale*.

Many of the solo effects on French organs came from the various mutation stops that they possessed. These would normally include a Cornet stop of four or five ranks on the Grande Orgue, consisting of 8 foot, 4 foot, $2\frac{2}{3}$ foot, 2 foot and $1\frac{3}{5}$ foot ranks. The Tierce rank, of $1\frac{3}{5}$ foot pitch, gave the characteristic edge to the stop. In order to help the sound carry, the Cornet stop was often mounted on its own small windchest above the rest of the pipework, with wind conveyanced to it through metal tubes. The Mounted Cornet was also found in Germanic and English organs during the seventeenth and eighteenth centuries.

The Cornet stop on a French organ would often be combined with the reed stops on the Grande Orgue, along with the 4 foot principal, to produce a full brassy sound, called the *Grand Jeu*. The *Plein Jeu*, on the other hand, comprised the flue stops of the Grande Orgue and the Positif.

Stop registration on French organs of the seventeenth and eighteenth centuries was very stylised. A composer who marked the score with, for example, the words 'Grand Jeu', would know that the organist would understand that he had to draw certain stops and that the sound would be much the same, regardless of which instrument was being played. Solo stops or combinations of stops were indicated in much the same way. The phrase '*Tierce en taille*', for example, meant that the Tierce rank (usually voiced as a flute rather than a principal stop) would be played with 8, 4, 2 and perhaps $1\frac{1}{3}$ foot stops in the bottom half of its compass, accompanied on the Positif manual by 8 foot and possibly 4 foot flute stops. The conventions of French organ playing are discussed more fully in chapter 3.

Many French organs built before 1800 still survive, despite the French Revolution and an extensive rebuilding programme in the nineteenth century. The organ at Le Petit Andely, near Rouen in northern France, built in 1674 by Ingout, is a good example of the classical French organ, both in tonal design and appearance. Some eighteenth-century builders attempted to combine elements of the French and German instruments into one organ. The large four-manual organ built by Riepp at Ottobeuren Abbey, Bavaria, in 1761–6 combines German choruses with French solo stops, for example.

Organs in Spain, Portugal and Italy

Spanish and Portuguese organs developed in a different way from either French or Germanic instruments. Many of the earlier Iberian organs were constructed by Flemish builders. While they had the same basic stoplists as the kind of organ already discussed, the emphasis was on powerful reed stops, often mounted

Ottobeuren, Germany: (left) the Trinity organ, c.1761–6; (right) the 'Holy Ghost' organ, c.1761.

The Epistle organ of Granada Cathedral, Spain, 1745–7. This case faces into the choir; there is another equally ornate case at the back. Some of the smaller case pipes are dummies. Note the Rückpositiv and the many horizontal or 'en chamade' reed pipes.

horizontally (*en chamade*) at the front of the instrument. These were used for special occasions and as a way of helping the sound to travel throughout the building. Placing the reeds in this position also meant that the reed tongues did not easily gather dust and the ranks could be tuned more readily than where the pipes were placed upright. Almost all the stops in an Iberian organ are divided between bass and treble halves so that there are two stopknobs for each rank. This allowed solo and accompanimental combinations of stops to be used on the same manual.

The Pedal division was usually less well developed than in German instruments and the third and fourth manuals controlled small divisions intended for echo or solo effects, as in French organs. Spanish and Portuguese church instruments were often placed in the arches on either side of what in an English church would be called the chancel (where the choir sits). There might well be an organ on both sides, and these instruments could be used antiphonally. It is now thought that the very first Swell divisions appeared in Spanish organs early in the eighteenth century. These swell organs were of short compass and contained only a few stops.

Italian organs from the sixteenth to the nineteenth centuries remained small, consisting normally of one manual with pedal pull-downs (that is, the pedals activated the lower keys of the manual rather than any independent pedal pipes). These instruments nevertheless included a wide range of stops – flue, reed, open, stopped. The reed stops were often placed at the front in order to provide easy

The organ of Saragossa (Zaragoza) Cathedral, Spain. The main case — on two levels — is fifteenth-century. The horizontal reeds were added in the eighteenth century.

A pair of organs either side of the choir in Milan Cathedral. The north organ was built in 1552; the south organ was built to match it in 1583–1610. Each case has two fronts, like the Granada organ.

access for tuning purposes. From the fifteenth until the eighteenth century the normal practice was to separate all the ranks on the windchest, even those of the highest pitch, which in other countries would form part of the mixture stops. This no doubt helped the organist to provide a wider range of sounds than would otherwise be possible from a small instrument. A small number of very large organs were built in Italy in the eighteenth century, culminating in instruments such as that at Catania in Sicily in 1755. This organ had five manuals, three consoles and fifty-five stops. However, it was really several different organs combined rather than a single large instrument.

Registration in the Italian organ was highly stylised, with different stops or combinations of stops being used to accompany each part of the Catholic mass, for which the Italian organ was primarily designed. The full organ, for example, would be used for slow, sustained and dignified music, as befitted the end of the service.

The English organ

Little is known about the development of the pipe organ in England from the building of the instrument in Winchester Cathedral in AD *c*.990 until the early sixteenth century. Given the Benedictine order's interest in music and organs, there

The organ at Adlington Hall, Cheshire, played by Handel in 1741 and 1751. It is not known who built the instrument, but it is thought to date from c.1690. The organ was unplayable for many years but was restored by Noel Mander in 1959. The two manual divisions are on a single windchest. The display pipes immediately above the keyboards are dummies. The front pipes are made of polished tin.

St John's College, Cambridge. Four-manual organ by N. P. Mander, 1994, incorporating some pipework from the previous instrument, including the horizontal Trompeta Real.

must have been organs in at least some of their other churches and cathedrals in England before the Reformation. There are occasional references in surviving medieval documents to the installation or the restoration of instruments (York Minster in 1147, Westminster Abbey in 1304). In many cases more than one instrument is mentioned, suggesting that organs were placed in various parts of the church to accompany different services or different parts of the same service, as at Durham Cathedral, where there were at least five instruments in use before the Reformation. It is also known that organ builders from continental Europe worked in England in the fifteenth and sixteenth centuries. In 1457, for example, a Dutch friar named John Roose is said to have built an organ for York Minster. By the fifteenth century there was a Guild of 'Orgelmakers', though this was dissolved in 1531.

The earliest significant documentation concerning organ building in England dates from 1519. In that year Antony Duddington built an organ for All Hallows Church, Barking, Essex, with a standard manual compass for the time of twenty-seven natural keys (white notes) and a full principal chorus. Whether or not the principal ranks could be separated by stops is not known. There may have been stopped bass pipes, possibly played by pedals, as in continental organs of the period.

A few sixteenth- and early-seventeenth-century English organ cases survive (Framlingham, Suffolk; King's College, Cambridge; Old Radnor, Powys; Tewkesbury Abbey, Gloucestershire) but little is known about their original contents. The construction and ornamentation of the cases suggest both French and Dutch/Flemish influences. Records of instruments built in England later in the sixteenth century suggest that the specifications were closer to Italian styles than French or Germanic ones. As far as can be determined, few if any English organs built in either the fifteenth or the sixteenth century had pedals. Mixtures were rarely included until the 1660s and all the ranks, however small, could be controlled separately, as in Italy. Reed stops were also rare until the seventeenth century, even though the regal was a popular instrument at the Tudor and

The Thomas Thamar organ now in St Michael's Church, Framlingham, Suffolk. The organ was originally built for Pembroke College, Cambridge, and transferred to Framlingham when a new instrument was built in the eighteenth century. The case is reputedly pre-Restoration.

45

A reconstruction by Goetze & Gwynn, 2001, of the Wingfield organ. All the pipes are of wood. The instrument would have been used to alternate with voices in the singing of plainchant.

Elizabethan courts. The Early English Organ Project oversaw the reconstruction in 2002 of two organs based on fragments of windchests from instruments thought to have been used at Wingfield and Wetheringsett churches in Suffolk during the 1520s. This has given us a much clearer idea of how pre-Reformation English church organs sounded and were used in the liturgy.

Larger English organs often had two manuals. There are many references to the construction of 'double organs' and, indeed, compositions such as the *Voluntaries for Double Organ* by John Lugge, organist of Exeter Cathedral early in the seventeenth century, require a two-manual organ but do not need pedals. Many of these two-manual instruments had Great and Chair divisions, as in the organ built by Dallam for Worcester Cathedral in 1613. Sometimes the second division was placed inside the main case with the Great organ. A large English organ built in the 1690s, though probably by a continental builder, survives at Adlington Hall, Cheshire. There are two manuals, a large Great division with each rank separable from the others, and a small Choir division of only three stops placed inside the main case and sharing its Stopped Diapason pipes with those of the Great division. There are three reed stops and there is a suggestion that at some point an attempt was made to fit pedal pull-downs.

During the Commonwealth period (1649–60) most church organs were either destroyed or removed from their original location. The organ at Magdalen College, Oxford, built some time after 1615, was presented to Oliver Cromwell, who had the instrument removed in 1654 to Hampton Court, where the poet Milton is said to have played it. The organ was returned to Oxford in 1661. It was moved to Tewkesbury Abbey in 1737. Some instruments were stored away for protection until the Restoration of the Monarchy; others were moved into taverns to accompany the singing there!

Between the end of the English Civil War and the Restoration of the Monarchy, a number of English organ builders worked in northern France. Here they were influenced by the French style of organ building and brought new ideas back to

The organ of Oriel College, Oxford, built in 1988 by J.W.Walker, with twenty stops and mechanical action. The case was made by Christopher Shrider in 1716 for the organ of St Mary Abbots, Kensington, London. The pipework is modelled on the Shrider organ at Finedon, Northamptonshire.

Below: *The organ of East Dereham Parish Church, Norfolk, rebuilt by Richard Bower. The instrument is a good example of enlargement over the years. It began life as a one-manual chamber organ (all with wooden pipes) built by 'Father' Smith. It was then rebuilt in the nineteenth century by Holt and then again by Hill; restored in the twentieth century by Hill, Norman & Beard and then enlarged again. Note the new Chair organ in the Gothick style.*

England with them in the 1660s, when organs were once more allowed in churches and organ builders were in demand. Foremost amongst the French-influenced builders was Renatus Harris (c.1652–1724), one of a long line of English organ builders. Few of his organs survive in their original form, even though by the time of his death in 1724 he had built at least six organs for cathedrals and many more for parish churches. His largest organ was at Salisbury Cathedral, where the instrument had four manuals, though the fourth keyboard controlled only a selection of stops from the Great division. The organ may have had pedal pull-downs.

Bernard Smith (c.1630–1708) was Harris's arch-rival. The two organ builders even contested a 'battle of organs' at the Temple Church in London, to see which of them should

The organ of St James, Clerkenwell, London, a two-manual organ. Case and some pipework by George Pike England, 1792; restored by Noel Mander, 1978.

receive the contract to build an organ for that prestigious church. Smith won, perhaps because he introduced many ranks new to England from Germany and Holland, where it is thought that he trained as an organ builder. His most famous instrument was at St Paul's Cathedral, built between 1695 and 1697. He was named 'Father' Smith to denote his premier position in English organ building of the period and perhaps to differentiate him from others with the same name.

Smith and Harris introduced mixtures, cornets, mutations and reed stops into English organs as standard parts of the specification. Apart from a few instances where pedal pull-downs were included, there was no pedal division and no pedal keyboard. The manual keyboards were longer than on the continent, with four or more additional notes at the bass end of the manuals. This would help the organist to provide depth to the sound in the absence of pedal pipes. The Great and Chair or Choir divisions were the norm until the end of the eighteenth century. Third manuals were normally called Echo in late-seventeenth- and early-eighteenth-century English organs. The Echo division was normally of short compass, like the French organ's Récit manual. On occasion this division was enclosed in a box to make the sound more distant. Swell shutters were introduced early in the eighteenth century, probably by Abraham Jordan in his instrument for St Magnus the Martyr, London Bridge. Jordan imported sherry from Spain, where he is thought to have discovered the idea for swell shutters of some kind. Early swell mechanisms were operated by a rope fitted to a pedal near the player's feet. The lever that operated the shutters in front of the box itself looked like a child's hobby-horse, hence the nickname 'nag's head swell', which is often given to early swell mechanisms.

Apart from the introduction of the Swell division and mechanism, English organ building followed much the same style as that created by Harris and Smith, remaining relatively small (maximum three manuals and twenty-five stops), with no pedals and few, if any, manual couplers. The Chair division, as on the continent, gradually disappeared, being replaced by a division in the main case of the instrument. These changes apart, an organ built at the end of the eighteenth century in England would have been easily recognisable to a late-seventeenth-century organ builder, at least in terms of the stoplist, if not the actual sound.

A small number of organ builders dominated English organ building in the eighteenth century. Only the larger churches and cathedrals possessed organs, though these were often a matter of much local pride and occasionally dispute. When John Snetzler (1710–85), a Swiss organ builder who spent most of his working life in England, built a large organ for Halifax Parish Church, West Yorkshire, in 1764–6, many of the local townspeople boycotted its use, claiming that it was too expensive. It took two years of wrangling in the ecclesiastical courts before the instrument could be used!

The organ at Halifax was typical of those instruments built in English churches and cathedrals during the late seventeenth and eighteenth centuries. It replaced a small band that had previously led the singing of the services. In smaller country churches, many of these bands continued into the nineteenth century, though virtually all had been wound up by 1850. Thomas Hardy's novel *Under the Greenwood*

GREAT ORGAN		CHOIR ORGAN	
Open Diapason	8	Open Diapason	8
Open Diapason	8	Stopped Diapason	8
Stopped Diapason	8	Principal	4
Principal	4	Flute	4
Twelfth	3	Fifteenth	2
Fifteenth	2	Bassoon	8
Sesquialtera	IV	Vox Humana	8
Furniture	III		
Cornet	V	SWELL ORGAN	
Trumpet	8	Open Diapason	8
Clarion	4	Stopped Diapason	8
		Principal	4
		Sesquialtera	III
		Hautboy	8
		Trumpet	8

Tree tells the story of how a village church band was replaced by a pipe organ.

The Halifax Parish Church organ was placed on a gallery at the west end of the church. Its specification is shown above. There were no couplers or pedals. The compass of the Great and Choir manuals began three natural keys lower than present-day keyboards. The Swell division began sixteen natural keys above the bottom note on a modern manual keyboard. The swell shutters would be controlled by the nag's head movement referred to earlier. The Cornet stop, which had pipes only for the upper part of the keyboard, was mounted above the rest of the Great pipework on its own separate windchest. It complemented the Clarion, which was supplied with pipes only for the lower part of the compass. The Sesquialtera was a particular kind of mixture with a Tierce rank in its composition, the term denoting the relationship between that rank and the others in the stop. Hautboy is another name for Oboe. Though it is not included in the stoplist for Halifax, Snetzler is credited with the introduction of the Dulciana stop into English organs. The Dulciana is a small-scaled, soft-toned Diapason or Principal stop, useful for accompanying the solo stops of other manuals.

The Halifax organ was extensively rebuilt in the nineteenth and twentieth centuries and now contains only a few pipes from the original organ. The first organist was William Herschel, who later became Astronomer Royal.

The organ in America

Organs were erected in America as early as the sixteenth century. These instruments were imported from Spain and Portugal for the cathedrals and monasteries of the Iberian colonies. A number of eighteenth-century instruments are reputed to exist still in the remoter parts of South America in particular. Organs imported from France existed in Quebec churches as early as 1657. A number of organs were brought from Germany to Pennsylvania in the eighteenth century by the colonists there, and a similar import of organs from England took place in New England at the same time. All these instruments were small.

St Paul, Honiton, Devon. Organ by Kenneth Tickell & Co. A new two-manual instrument on a specially constructed west gallery. The oak casework is modelled on Italianate lines, with the Great, Swell and Pedal divisions all speaking from behind the front pipes. The Great is at impost level (that is, at the level of the lower pipes) and the Swell is above, in the upper part of the case. The Pedal pipes are on either side. The instrument has mechanical action and electric registration aids.

By *c.*1750 organs were being built in North America, in eastern Pennsylvania and Boston. Pennsylvanian organs followed German models, while those built in Boston were copies of English eighteenth-century instruments. It was not until well into the nineteenth century that organ builders in America adopted the more modern styles and techniques of construction and tonal design then prevalent in Europe. From then on, however, a significant number of larger instruments were constructed by American builders.

The organ after 1800

By the beginning of the nineteenth century organ-building styles were starting to change. Composers such as Beethoven, Berlioz and Liszt sought vivid means of expression. The Werkprinzip organ in particular gave way to instruments that aimed to provide the organist with an orchestra at his fingertips. Organ builders placed greater emphasis on extremes of sound and an ability to build up tone

The author with the 'nag's head swell' mechanism of the Wymondham Abbey organ.

colours from combinations of 8 and 4 foot stops. Solo registers became more important than chorus ranks in many instruments. Because of its capacity for dynamic change, the swell box increased in importance during the course of the nineteenth century. More and more of the stops and the divisions were enclosed. In some cases the whole instrument was placed in a swell box.

These changes in the tonal design and layout of the organ were common throughout Europe. The Werkprinzip tradition was maintained to a certain extent in the Germanic countries where it had always been most influential, with fewer stops being enclosed than in instruments elsewhere. Organs became larger and louder, nevertheless.

In France organ building in the nineteenth century was dominated by Aristide Cavaillé-Coll, who built or rebuilt most of the major instruments in that country between 1841 and the end of the century. He continued the emphasis placed on reed stops by earlier French builders and introduced new varieties of stop such as

the Gamba and the Celeste. However, he retained the chorus and some of the mutation stops of the eighteenth-century French organ. A great many of Cavaillé-Coll's instruments remain much as he left them. The largest relatively unaltered organ is at the basilica of St Sulpice, Paris. Charles-Marie Widor played here for many years. The Cavaillé-Coll organ at St Clotilde, Paris, is said to have inspired its organist, César Franck, to produce some of the finest music for the instrument composed in the nineteenth century.

The eighteenth-century English tradition continued for a time, though gradually English organ

The organ of Trinity College, Dublin, Ireland, built by J. W. Walker & Sons in 1967 (originally by Samuel Green c.1790). It is a three-manual organ with twenty-five stops and mechanical action.

Magdalene College, Cambridge. Organ by Goetze & Gwynn, 2000. A modern interpretation of a classical English organ style, with Great and Chair divisions. There is no Swell section and only a small Pedal division. The compasses are modern, however. There are obvious similarities with the Dublin organ on page 52.

The organ at Bolton Town Hall, Lancashire. Built by J.W.Walker & Sons in 1985, it has four manuals, forty-three stops and mechanical action. The organ replaced an earlier instrument destroyed by fire.

Greyfriars Kirk, Edinburgh. Three-manual organ by Peter Collins, 1990. Note the modern interpretation of the Werkprinzip approach, complete with separate pedal towers and Back-Positive. There is also room for Spanish influences in the horizontal reeds.

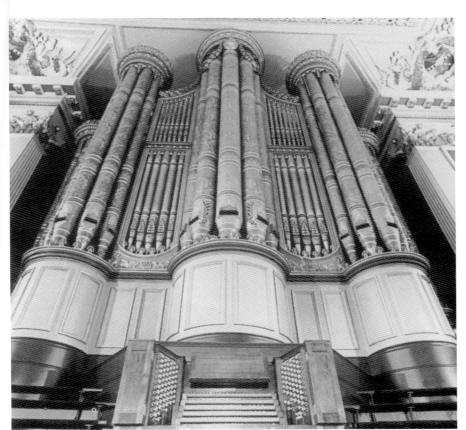

The organ by Noel Mander in Birmingham Town Hall, based on the William Hill organ of 1834, with additions in 1843, 1890 and 1933. The instrument was the first to contain a high-pressure solo reed. The instrument has since been reduced to four manuals, with the Bombarde division being a 'floating' one, capable of being played from some of the other keyboards.

builders adopted the styles and approaches of a whole range of continental European companies. Manual compasses were standardised and pedals added. For a short period from about 1840 to 1860 English organ builders led the field in tonal design. Through the work of H. J. Gauntlett, who studied organ building on the continent, and William Hill, one of the major English organ builders of the nineteenth century, a new kind of instrument emerged, capable of playing both the classical repertoire epitomised by the music of J. S. Bach and the new romantic compositions. The Hill/Gauntlett organ had complete choruses on the Great, Swell, Pedal and (to a lesser extent) Choir divisions, and a wide range of solo stops and mutations. Unlike many other English builders of the period, Hill respected older organs, rebuilding them sympathetically. Unfortunately many of his pioneering instruments have themselves been rebuilt. The Ulster Hall, Belfast, contains a large four-manual concert organ by Hill.

Hill built the first large town-hall organ at Birmingham in 1834. In 1840, he added a Tuba Mirabilis stop. This was the first example of a high-pressure solo reed,

Chichester Cathedral organ, largely by William Hill, 1851, 1859 and 1888, but based on earlier work by Harris and Byfield and restored by Noel Mander in 1985. It includes a 'nave' section. The smaller organ case is for the functional Chair organ.

Chestnut Hill Presbyterian Church, United States of America. Organ by N. P. Mander Ltd. A basic eighteenth-century English organ case design, developed into a Werkprinzip organ.

useful for solos against the rest of the organ stops and as a climax to the full organ. Stops like this were to become commonplace in English concert and cathedral organs, though the tradition very rarely seems to have been adopted abroad.

Most English town halls built in the nineteenth century had an organ installed in their concert auditorium. Many of these grand instruments still survive. The largest, at the Royal Albert Hall in London, has over 120 stops. Many of the ranks, and especially the reeds, are on high wind pressures. Originally built by Henry Willis, one of the great organ builders of the nineteenth century, the Albert Hall organ was rebuilt in the 1920s by the firm of Harrison & Harrison, one of the most renowned builders of the twentieth century. Concert-hall organs such as this have had to provide music for a wide range of functions, including interludes between boxing matches! Like Smith before him, Willis was called 'Father' as a mark of respect and also to differentiate him from his organ-building family, many of whom were also called Henry!

The town-hall organ came to the fore at a time when there were few orchestras and the only way in which people could hear symphonic music was through transcriptions for organ. The instrument was turned into a one-man band capable of synthesising the various parts of the orchestra. In later town-hall organs the stops included percussion effects such as drums, cymbals and bird whistles. There was nothing new in this: large seventeenth- and eighteenth-century organs in Germany, for instance, contained similar effects such as the Cymbelstern, as noted earlier.

The firms of Hill, Willis and Harrison & Harrison built or rebuilt most of the major concert, town-hall and cathedral organs in Britain. While their instruments retained the basic choruses of the eighteenth-century organ, they further developed solo stops and choruses of reeds. In particular, Willis developed the characteristic English 'full swell' effect: a chorus of powerful reeds at 16, 8 and 4 foot pitches, together with a Tierce mixture, all enclosed in a swell box. The most renowned of these full swells is that of the organ of St Paul's Cathedral in London.

The Schulze organ in St Bartholomew's Church, Armley, Leeds; four-manual, 1869.

English firms of the time were all influenced in different ways by some of the continental builders of the day, notably Cavaillé-Coll and the famous nineteenth-century German firm of Schulze. Schulze exported a number of instruments to Britain. The firm's flute stops, usually made of wood and often named Lieblich Gedackt when stopped, and powerful principal choruses made a considerable impact on British organ building for several generations. The Schulze organs at Doncaster Parish Church and St Bartholomew's Church, Armley, Leeds, remain much as the builder left them. Schulze himself is reputed to have been influenced by the work of the Silbermann family.

In order to assist the player to control larger instruments, organ builders invented tubular-pneumatic and electro-pneumatic actions, which lightened the key touch and enabled stops to be changed quickly. The very first pneumatic action, known as Barker lever after its inventor, C. S. Barker, combined tracker action with pneumatic motors that lightened the touch of the keys, especially when manuals were coupled together. A number of registration aids were also developed, many of them in England. In their crudest form such aids were simple shifting movements that shut off wind to certain stops, thus saving the organist the trouble of pushing or pulling the stopknobs in or out. In the early nineteenth century an English organ builder, J. C. Bishop, invented composition pedals. These were foot pedals, usually made of metal, which activated a series of levers that pushed out a particular group of stops. With electric and pneumatic actions, these pedals were replaced by pistons, which activated the stops either electrically or pneumatically. In his organ for the Great Exhibition of 1851 Henry Willis placed small pistons between the manual keys so that the organist could change stops while playing simply by pressing the pistons with his thumbs or fingers. Most modern organs have such registration aids. Where the mechanism is electrically controlled, the pistons can be changed at will by the organist by means of setter switches of various kinds attached to the piston system. Cinema organs in particular also have 'double-touch' systems, whereby the harder the key is depressed or the stop pulled or pushed, for example, the more stops are brought into use and the louder the sound. Foot pistons on French organs are called *champignons* because they look like mushrooms!

For much of the twentieth century the English cathedral organ, as built by Harrison & Harrison, was regarded as the ideal instrument, emulated the world over. Many cathedral and large church organs still follow the basic Harrison design, first used at Ely Cathedral in 1908. Probably the best known of the Harrison instruments is at King's College, Cambridge. The instrument is typical of many organs in Britain especially, having been rebuilt and enlarged several times.

North American organ builders emulated British and German makers from the 1870s onwards. The large organ of the Boston Music Hall, built by Walcker of Ludwigsburg, Germany, greatly influenced American organ builders, setting a trend for bigger instruments. A number of very large organs were built in North America in the nineteenth and twentieth centuries, including the largest organ in the world at Atlantic City, New Jersey, with seven manuals and over thirty thousand pipes.

Other types of organ

If the concert-hall organ was a development of the nineteenth century, then the cinema or theatre organ was a product of the twentieth century. Until films had soundtracks, there was a need for some form of accompaniment to complement the silent motion pictures that were shown in cinemas. The organ, as a one-man band, was the ideal instrument to provide such accompaniment. With electric action, the pipes could be fitted in anywhere around the auditorium. The theatre organ had a wide range of sounds and tone colours and an endless range of special effects, from bird whistles to thunder pedals and from foghorns to church bells, all of which could be used to enhance the drama of the film.

Initially, theatre and cinema organs were much the same as church or concert-hall instruments. A different and distinct style of design and construction soon emerged, however. The pioneer of the cinema organ was Robert Hope-Jones (1859–1914). He patented new forms of electric action and changed the organ's tonal design from one in which a series of choruses forms the basis of the sound to one where loud 16, 8 and 4 foot stops are the only ranks required. Hope-Jones also invented the *Diaphone*, a kind of reed stop of very pure tone. Because it could be made to sound very loud, the Diaphone was often used to make foghorns! Hope-Jones's first instruments were for churches, including a large four-manual instrument built for Worcester Cathedral in 1896. His mechanical inventions

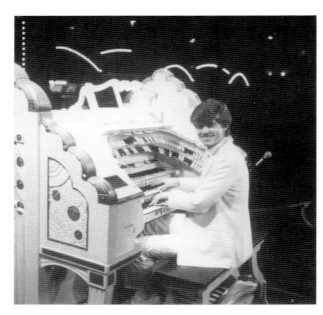

*Robert Wolfe at the
Wurlitzer cinema organ
at the Thursford
Collection, Norfolk.*

required a better supply of electricity than was generally available at the end of the nineteenth century and many of his instruments seem to have soon become unplayable. He survived bankruptcy, however, and emigrated to the United States, where his business interests were acquired by the Wurlitzer organ company, which developed Hope-Jones's ideas into the cinema organ.

In most cinema organs all the stops were enclosed in swell boxes as a means of maximising the expressive capabilities of the instrument. New ranks were developed. These included the Tibia, a large-scale, heavily-blown flute stop, and the Kinura, a keen-sounding reed rank. In order to increase the range of the instrument, each rank of pipes was extended over a number of pitches. Thus a register might appear at 16, 8, 4, $2\frac{2}{3}$, 2 and $1\frac{3}{5}$ foot pitches, and on more than one manual. The principle of extension of ranks was well known from the Renaissance onwards but it was especially used also in many church and concert organs in the first half of the twentieth century. The John Compton Organ Company was renowned for using this approach and even at the start of the twenty-first century extension is used for pedal stops, where only one note at a time is typically being played. Pedal stops are also 'borrowed' from the manuals and stops 'duplexed' from one manual to another in these schemes.

The characteristic sound of the cinema organ comes from the use of the Tremulant. While in most church and concert-hall organs the Tremulant is used only occasionally, usually in combination with a solo stop or stops, the Tremulants on a cinema organ are in almost constant use. They are intended to provide the equivalent of the vibrato on a stringed instrument.

Once 'talking' films arrived, the cinema organ lost its popularity and in the 1950s and 1960s many instruments were removed from their original homes and often

The chamber organ at Carisbrooke Castle, Isle of Wight, by Hoffheimer, 1602. Reputedly played by Princess Elizabeth, daughter of King Charles I, this organ can still be played today.

scrapped altogether. Some have been rebuilt in new surroundings, where they are still regularly used. The organ museum at Thursford, Norfolk, houses one of the largest cinema organs still playable in Britain. One of the few cinema organs remaining in its original home is that built by Wurlitzer for the Tower Ballroom, Blackpool. Like many cinema organs, the instrument has a 'resident' organist. Reginald Dixon was for many years organist there, though, unlike many of his fellow organists, he accompanied dancing rather than films.

Pipe organs were also found in private houses. The organ had long been a secular instrument, and there are references to organs at the courts of medieval and Renaissance monarchs and in the homes of princes and rich merchants. Such organs were always small. There would normally be only a limited amount of space to house the instrument and the music played on these house organs would not be complex — they were for the owners rather than professional musicians to play. The organ at Adlington Hall, Cheshire, referred to earlier, was larger than most. Much more typical is the small instrument in Carisbrooke Castle, Isle of Wight. Built at the end of the sixteenth century by a continental organ builder, it is the oldest playable organ in Britain. It has no pedals, one manual of a relatively short compass of forty-five notes and three stops: flute ranks of 4 foot and 2 foot pitch and an 8 foot Regal.

Many house or chamber organs were built in the eighteenth century and a good many instruments survive in country houses. Many were built in Britain by the main church-organ builders such as Smith, Harris and Snetzler. These instruments

The chest organ at Osterley Park, Middlesex. The instrument was built by White in 1788 on behalf of the organ builder Henry Holland — an early example of contracting out of labour. The instrument is in the form of a chest and the pipes are in the base of the instrument. Its compactness means that it can be moved if necessary. The pipes are all of wood.

usually had only one manual and no pedals, a principal chorus up to 2 foot pitch, a Cornet stop and possibly a solo reed rank. A number of the stops would draw in two parts so that, even though the organ had only one keyboard, a solo could be played with the right hand by drawing only the upper part of the stop.

Chamber organs would be used for private practice and entertainment. Small organs were also used in churches on the continent to accompany small services or as part of the orchestra, fulfilling the continuo role, filling out the instrumental parts. Just as people demonstrated their wealth by building large church or concert-hall organs, so many rich people installed organs in their own homes. The Schulze organ now at Armley, for instance, though a large four-manual instrument with a bold principal chorus, was originally a house organ.

Some organs have no pipes at all. In the late twentieth century the electronic – and more recently the digital – organ has developed, in which sounds are produced like those of an instrument with pipes but by electronic or digital means. The advantage of these organs is that they save space and, though they have a shorter life than a well-made pipe organ, they need less maintenance. Electronic and digital organs are popular as house instruments, though even here there is now a renaissance in pipe-organ construction. The most up-to-date digital instruments can produce a wide range of sounds at the touch of a button and sound very much

A four-manual electronic organ by Copeman Hart. The lack of pipes means that even the largest organs can be fitted into small spaces.

like real pipe organs. Some pipe organs now have digital stops, especially where space is at a premium and there is no room for large ranks such as 32 foot reeds.

The 'American organ' and harmonium have no pipes, except perhaps dummy ones. Their characteristic reedy sound is made from small reeds inside the instrument. In a sense, they are the descendant of the regal, described earlier. In Britain, the harmonium became very popular as a house instrument and in small churches and chapels. It still survives in some country churches as the only accompaniment to services.

Some organs have pipes but no keyboards. Mechanical organs, most familiar as barrel organs, have been made for several centuries. Queen Elizabeth I sent the royal organ builder, Dallam, to Turkey to build a mechanical organ for the Sultan. The principle is the same as with a standard pipe organ. The difference is that, instead of keyboards and fingers, the instrument is played by a mechanical device that pulls the pallets under the windchest at the right time. Typically, a barrel with spikes or holes in it matches up with the mechanism of the instrument. Each spike or hole corresponds to a note on the instrument and whenever it comes round on the barrel the note plays. In fairground organs the pallets are activated by folding cards with perforations that correspond to the notes of music. Some of the holes activate stop changes. There were many barrel organs in churches in the nineteenth century simply because there was no organist. The illustration on page 73 shows a barrel and finger organ, with both mechanical and human options possible. Some music was written especially for mechanical organs. Haydn wrote pieces, for example, while Mozart composed two large-scale fantasias for the instrument, though they are such grand compositions that they must have strained the mechanism and are played nowadays by an organist. With the advent of digital transmission systems, pipe organs with keyboards can be played automatically and the organist can record his performance for future playback.

Modern organ design

Since the 1960s organ builders have returned to the styles of the seventeenth and eighteenth centuries, copying the Werkprinzip organs described earlier in this chapter. Many instruments are now built with tracker action and a stoplist similar to that used by J. S. Bach and his contemporaries. The organ at the Royal Festival Hall, London, was the first major British organ of the twentieth century to use eighteenth-century stoplists and pipe voicing, though the action was electro-pneumatic rather than tracker and, unlike an eighteenth-century organ, there was no proper casework. The organ at Queen's College, Oxford, built by the Danish organ builder Frobenius, was the first truly Werkprinzip organ built in Britain. Such organs have been built again in Germany since the 1920s, when Albert Schweitzer, amongst others, drew attention to the many old organs still surviving. Schweitzer persuaded organ builders to return to eighteenth-century styles of organ design and construction. The resulting neo-classical type of organ has been adopted as the model for church and concert-hall organs in Europe and North America. In France there has also been a return to the styles of the eighteenth century, though the work of Cavaillé-Coll has also been preserved. The remaining

The organs of Chelmsford Cathedral, built by N. P. Mander Ltd, 1995. The large west-end organ (top) has four manuals. A separate east-end instrument was constructed to accompany the choir (too far removed from the west end). This east-end instrument (bottom) can also control most of the west-end organ. Both instruments have mechanical key action.

Above left: *A modern organ built in 1989 by Peter Collins, Leicester, after the style of the Strasbourg Silbermanns, for the International Organ Festival, St Albans.*

Above right: *The modern house organ at Chalfont Heights, Buckinghamshire, built in 1973 by Peter Collins.*

historic organs in Britain are gradually being carefully restored to their original condition wherever possible and are also used increasingly as models for new instruments. Much work remains to be done to restore the classical organs of Spain, Portugal and Italy.

Pipe organs are still regularly built or rebuilt throughout the world. Large organs of over one hundred stops have been built in countries as far apart as the United States, Australia and Hong Kong. At the other end of the scale, small one- or two-manual instruments, with only a few stops, are also still built in many churches, schools, concert rooms and homes.

An organ by N. P. Mander Ltd for a private customer in New Jersey, United States of America. Note the return to eighteenth-century styles of casework.

Under construction in 1989 at the factory of J.W.Walker & Sons at Brandon, Suffolk, is an organ for the church of St Martin-in-the-Fields, London. The organ follows the Werkprinzip arrangement of divisions and stops.

3
Technique and repertoire

Technique

Unlike any other musical instrument, the organ can sustain sound indefinitely. A note played on a piano will die away as the string inside the instrument gradually stops vibrating after being struck by the hammer attached to the key. A note played on a woodwind or brass instrument will sound only as long as the player has breath in his or her lungs. But an organ pipe will sound without any loss of power or change in timbre until the player chooses to stop depressing the manual or pedal key.

Because of this sustaining quality the playing technique required for the organ is markedly different from that for both the harpsichord and the piano. In order to make a smooth transition from one note to another, the organist must ensure that there is neither too great nor too small a gap between the point where wind stops entering one pipe and the point where wind enters the next. In many cases the player must change fingers or feet while depressing the same key or pedal in order to ensure a smooth sound.

An organist has only two feet (as opposed to ten fingers) so that, while many notes can be played on the manuals at the same time, only two or, at most, three notes can be depressed by either the toe or the heel of the foot at any one point. The same principle of smooth playing applies to the pedal part as to the manual parts of a piece of music. The organist has to learn to play the correct pedal notes without looking down at the feet. This takes time and a good deal of practice, though eventually it becomes second nature in the way that changing gear on a car is an automatic procedure, carried out without thinking by the experienced driver.

The player has to be able to co-ordinate the hands and feet so that, for example, three different melodies can be played at the same time – one in the right hand, the second in the left hand and the third in the pedals. Trio sonatas such as those by J. S. Bach require this complete independence of the hands and feet.

An important aspect of playing the organ is the selection and manipulation of the stops – the art of registration, as it is called. Organs vary considerably in size and tonal design, and the location of the instrument can have an important effect on the sound. In large churches, for instance, there may be an echo of several seconds after a pipe has ceased to sound. This has to be taken into account when playing if the music is not to sound so blurred that it becomes unrecognisable.

Because a pipe sounds the moment air is let into its foot and stops sounding as soon as the pallet closes, the organist has to take great care when adding or subtracting stops. In general, the registration is not altered while the stops on which the music is being played are sounding, but stops can be changed on one or more divisions while music is being played on another.

On a piano the player increases or decreases the volume by depressing the keys (and hence hitting the strings) with more or less force as appropriate. The only ways in which the volume can be increased or decreased on the organ are either to add or reduce the number of stops in use or to use the swell box, where available.

In practice, both techniques are often used together.

The way in which the sound is built up or reduced will depend on the particular instrument, the specification and the way in which the stops are voiced. In organ music written before about 1850 gradations in power normally take the form of a series of steps up or down in volume, given the Werkprinzip design of most instruments and the lack of swell boxes of any size. Indeed, much music would be played throughout on the same stop combinations. Because of the lack of registration aids and the cumbersome size of the stopknobs, an assistant would be required for rapid changes of stops in many cases.

Music written after 1850 places much more emphasis on finely graded crescendos and diminuendos, which can be properly achieved only with larger swell boxes and combination pedals or pistons. With a Swell division or divisions, even unenclosed ranks can seem to increase or decrease in volume if they are coupled to ranks that are enclosed. The organist's skill in gradually building up or reducing the volume is in knowing which ranks to add or subtract and at what point to open or close the swell box or boxes.

The registration of a piece of music will be determined not only by the instrument on which it is to be played but also by the historic conventions associated with the composition, as well as the player's personal taste and approach. We can only guess how early organs sounded and therefore do not know for certain which stops to use for the music that would have been played on them. However, where instruments survive that are contemporary with a particular composer or a school of composition, it is important to discover how they were used in order to give as authentic a performance as possible on other instruments.

Chapter 2 described the various styles of organ building. Until the eighteenth century it was virtually unknown for a piece of organ music to contain any instructions regarding the registration to be used. However, we do know with some degree of certainty how music from *c*.1680 onwards was to be registered. To a certain extent the instrument's limitations dictated the way in which the stops were used. Instruments were hand-blown and the channels through which the wind was led from the bellows to the windchest were often narrow. It would not normally be possible, therefore, to use all the stops together – there simply would not be enough wind for them all!

In any case, it is not necessary for all the registers to sound together in order to increase the volume. If a loud stop is added to a softer stop, then the sound of the softer stop is masked. Even if two stops of the same volume are added together, the sound output does not double in volume.

Increasing the power of the registration normally comes from adding stops of different pitches. Only one stop of each pitch is required in any combination of stops unless flue and reed stops are to be used together or there is a specific reason to make an exception to this convention. In many organs the largest pipes of the main principal rank on the Great and possibly Pedal divisions are often displayed in the front of the case. The air has to be brought specially to these ranks from tubes conveyanced off the main windchest. This tends to make the pipes speak less quickly than those on the windchest itself. In order to improve responsiveness, a

St Augustine's Church, Birdbrook, Essex. Organ by Rodney Briscoe. The use of electro-pneumatic action means that the pipes — but not the console — can be in the west tower arch.

second 8 foot stop (typically a stopped rank) on the main windchest is often added to the rank whose pipes are in the case. This usually covers up any irregularities in the sound. We also saw in chapter 1 how two 8 foot stops are deliberately made out of tune with each other in order to give a 'beating' effect.

Unless a special and unusual effect is being sought, the basis of any combination will be an 8 foot stop on the manual and a 16 foot stop on the pedal. 16 foot stops are often found on manual divisions and, when used, can add depth and grandeur to the sound. Conversely, using pedal stops of 8 foot pitch and above without a 16 foot or a 32 foot stop being added lightens the sound and provides a contrast to the normal pedal combinations. 4 foot stops are occasionally used on their own (some very small instruments do not have an 8 foot stop on all the manuals) or in combination with other higher-pitched stops. Above 4 foot pitch, stops are used only in combination with lower-pitched ranks, either as part of a chorus of principals or flutes, or to 'colour' the lower ranks to form a sound combination that will enable a solo melody to be played. Mutation stops (described in earlier chapters) are used in this way. Single stops, normally of 8 foot pitch, can also be used on their own for softer sounds. Stops on the same division can be combined with each other or with stops on other manuals and the pedals, using couplers, where available.

Where the music is chordal (where several notes are played at the same time), the stops used tend to be either the full flue chorus, with or without the reed stops, or possibly the reed stops on their own, or (in some circumstances) the 8 foot principal or Diapason stops alone. Such stop combinations can also be used for contrapuntal music, where one or more tunes are combined in different ways. However, in order to ensure that the tune or tunes can be clearly heard at all times,

Dickleburgh Parish Church, Norfolk. Appearances can be deceptive: organ and console are some 50 feet (15 metres) away from each other.

the organist has to ensure that the combination of stops used produces a clear sound. This is normally best done by using stops of the same kind (as for example the principal stops) at different pitches.

In trio sonatas (already referred to) and similar music where two or more different melodies are combined, it is important to ensure that each melody 'stands out' as it is being played. The organist will therefore use contrasting stops, on different manuals and the pedals, for each melodic line. One hand, for example, might be playing on a manual controlling a reed stop, the other on a manual controlling two flute stops of different pitches, while the pedals are controlling a single 8 foot principal stop. These stops should be different in timbre but approximately equal in volume.

In much organ music, however, one melody is meant to be heard more prominently than the others. Organs have a range of solo stops and solo combinations for this purpose. Indeed, as we saw in chapter 1, large instruments usually have a whole division of such ranks. The accompaniment will be played on another manual and the pedals, using softer flute, string or principal stops expressly voiced for the purposes.

One of the earliest known registration instructions is *organo pleno* or 'full organ'. The nature and sound of 'full organ' varies according to country and style of organ building. On one instrument it is possible to have more than one 'full organ' sound. The 'full organ' of the classical Werkprinzip instrument as played by J. S. Bach would normally consist of the full principal chorus on the main manual (Hauptwerk), with the full principal chorus on the pedals, plus the pedal reeds. In large instruments the main manuals might be coupled together for the *organo pleno*. To provide a contrast to this sound, parts of the piece might be played on a subsidiary chorus of stops on another division. The 'full organ' sound might be coloured with reed stops on the manual divisions, especially if the music were chordal rather than contrapuntal, and with any principal-scaled mutation ranks or Cornet stops.

In chapter 2 reference was made to the registration conventions of the French organ before about 1840. Here, full organ would be described as the 'Plein Jeu'. This would usually consist of the principal chorus on the Great division (Grande Orgue), possibly coupled to the principal chorus on the Positif, known as the 'Petit Plein Jeu'. Alternatively, the 'full organ' might consist of the 'Grand Jeu'. Here, the loud reeds on the Grande Orgue (or possibly the Bombarde division, if one existed) would be drawn along with the 4 foot Principal stop and the Cornet. The Cornet would help to maintain the power of the reed stops in the upper part of their compass. A French organist would know which stops to use when he saw one or other of these terms written in the music. Indeed, some of the titles of the pieces refer to the registration, as for example 'Offertoire sur les Grands Jeux'.

Because French organs of the late seventeenth and the eighteenth centuries were all built according to the same design, it was possible to develop standard registration instructions for music played on them. At the head of much French organ music of this period is a phrase (for example, 'Grand Jeu') that would mean the same to any French organist, whichever organ he was playing. Registration

Walpole St Peter, Norfolk. A new organ by Rodney Briscoe in an antique style. The Great is above the Swell, with the Pedal on either side.

instructions, apart from those for full organ, included directions on which stops to draw for a Trumpet or Cornet solo or a combination of mutation stops that included a Twelfth, Seventeenth and possibly a Nineteenth rank, or other reed- and flue-stop solos or combinations.

Similar registration instructions or conventions can be found in English organ music of the same period. The term 'Full Organ', for example, would result in the player drawing the Open and Stopped Diapasons, the Principal, Twelfth, Fifteenth and all Mixture stops on the Great Organ. If specially instructed, and there was enough wind, the Trumpet and Clarion stops would also be added. The manuals would not normally be coupled together. The term 'Diapasons' would instruct the player to use the Open and Stopped Diapasons together. Other directions would tell the organist which solo stop to use (for example, Trumpet, Flute, Vox Humana) or occasionally which manual to play on (for example, Swell or Echo).

In general, however, references to particular stops or stop combinations before about 1850 are rare. Very few of J. S. Bach's organ compositions contain any registration instructions and these may well not be original. It is clear from the

Barrel and finger organ, North Lopham Church, Norfolk. When an organist is available, the keyboard can be used; when a player is not to be found, the barrel is activated to play the instrument mechanically. Each barrel will contain several hymn or psalm tunes. Note the cranking handle on the right-hand side of the barrel.

texture of the music that some pieces require balanced combinations on each division while others need a solo stop or stops with accompaniment. Pedal solos would normally use stops of 8 foot or 4 foot pitch. Reed stops were often available at these pitches; their penetrating sound enables them to be more easily heard against the manual stops than a flute or a principal rank would be. In the larger compositions, and especially the Fugues written by Bach and his contemporaries, organists need to decide whether or not to change manuals during the course of the piece. There is no single correct interpretation of this question, and the decision whether or not to perform one or more sections on a second manual, alternating with the main one, will vary from piece to piece and instrument to instrument.

When performing older organ compositions, organists must also be aware of conventions relating to the playing of the notes themselves. Because music had to be written out by hand, a kind of musical shorthand developed to save time. Organists would know what was intended by the composer, even though not all the notes or rhythms were written out in full. The conventions used in this musical shorthand varied from country to country and period to period. One of the best known types of shorthand is the French system of *notes inégales* (unequal notes). Here, though the notation might seem to suggest that all the notes are played evenly, the convention of the time dictates that the notes should be played unevenly – not of equal length – the first note of a pair being longer than the second in the example given here.

After about 1850 composers of organ music became much more precise in their registration instructions. Many were players themselves and they often required a particular effect when their music was being performed. As in earlier periods, French organ registration was very stylised, especially since most of the major instruments were built or rebuilt by one person, Aristide Cavaillé-Coll. A direction to use the reeds or the full chorus on any instrument built by him would result in almost exactly the same sound being produced. His instruments were built on the understanding that different timbres would be produced by combining stops of the same pitch. The instruction 'Fonds' (foundation stops), for example, would direct the organist to use two, three or more 8 foot stops together. A gradual crescendo could be achieved by coupling the manuals together and either adding stops or having the stops already drawn, letting wind into them only when required. This

François Couperin: 'Messe pour les Paroisses'. Eighteenth-century French organ music was written and played according to certain specific conventions. One of these was the use of 'notes inégales'. Though written out as equal notes (left), the player would know to play the quavers of the piece as dotted quaver followed by semiquaver – as unequal notes (right).

Holy Trinity Church, Heigham, Norwich. The organ was built by Frederick Rothwell in 1921. The use of stop 'tabs' between the manuals meant that the stops could be changed quickly without the organist having to remove his hands from the keyboards. The system obviated the need for thumb pistons.

was possible through a ventil mechanism. The ventil was some form of block between the bellows and the part of the windchest that it controlled. With the ventil closed, wind would not reach the windchest and pipes would not sound, even if the stops had been drawn at the console and the sliders were correctly positioned over the windchest. With the ventil open, the wind could pass into the windchest and into any pipes whose sliders had been drawn.

In nineteenth-century German organs, crescendos and diminuendos were often achieved through a general crescendo pedal (*Rollschwelle*). As the pedal was depressed, the stops were added automatically, thus increasing the volume. Reversing the procedure reduced the sound. Much German organ music of the period relies on the organist's ability to move from the softest to the loudest combinations and back again.

Modern actions and registration aids (discussed in the two previous chapters) have enabled organists to change stops and sound levels or timbres rapidly. Certainly, when playing orchestral transcriptions or certain kinds of nineteenth- and twentieth-century organ music, the organist needs to be able to change registration quickly. This is a relatively straightforward operation when foot and thumb pistons are available, particularly when the stop combinations that they activate can be adjusted to suit the requirements of the piece being played. Through computer technology, modern organs can offer an almost infinite number of 'memories' on which piston settings can be left, including the complete sequence required for specific pieces of music.

Repertoire

Most organs of any size built before the nineteenth century were located in churches. The music written for these instruments was inevitably linked with the liturgy and the services of the type of church that had commissioned the building of the organ. The simple medieval organs would have accompanied or alternated with the plainchant singing, reinforcing the vocal lines. As instruments grew larger, more varied in tone and more sophisticated in operation, the organ became a solo as well as an accompanying instrument or an alternative to vocal music in the

Water organ, Villa d'Este, Tivoli, Italy. A new instrument was constructed in 2002 by Rodney Briscoe as a replica of the original sixteenth-century instrument. The bellows and the barrel mechanisms are driven by water.

South Acre Church, Norfolk. A nineteenth-century chamber organ. The front pipes are wooden dummies.

church services.

This section concentrates on the organ as a solo instrument. However, many organs today are still built to accompany singers, usually in church, and the pipes are constructed and voiced so that they can either accompany voices or other instruments or lead large congregations and choirs. The softer stops are useful for accompaniment, while the loud registers ensure that large numbers of singers are effectively supported. The principles of good accompanying are the same as those for effective solo playing: a sensitive approach to the music and the instrument; careful choice of registers, taking account of the organ, the building and the function; subtle change of stops when required; rhythmic playing and effective technique.

The church organ was used as a solo instrument in a number of ways. In the Roman Catholic mass it became customary for the organ to alternate with the singers or the priests in the performance of the plainsong. One section of the plainsong would be sung. The next would be played by the organist, who would embellish or vary the chant. The earliest variations would have been made up on the spot by the organist. The ability to improvise has remained an important part of the church organist's craft, for there are still many occasions during a service when music is required at short notice.

Much organ music is based on pre-existing melodies, whether plainsong, hymn melodies or other tunes, both secular and sacred. The *organ mass* consisted of a series of pieces that were to be played at various points in the communion service, normally in Catholic churches, and, as already noted, might alternate with singing. Some of the pieces in an organ mass would be based on plainsong – and especially those plainchant melodies that were sung during the course of the mass. The organ mass pieces embellished the plainsong tunes in the same way that German Protestant organists would embellish the chorale melodies as a prelude to the

Jan Sweelinck:Variations on 'Mein junges Leben hat ein End'. Some organ music — and especially compositions not written for a particular religious setting — is based on popular tunes, as in this example. This is a set of variations on the same tune. Each variation arranges the melody in a different way. Note for instance the difference between variations 1 and 5. In variation 5 the harmony remains the same as in variation 1; the melody is embellished considerably, however. The dynamic and speed markings are modern, as are the instructions to use particular manuals (Rp = Rückpositiv; Hw = Hauptwerk).

singing of the hymn. Organ mass and similar settings of plainsong, where the choir alternated with the organist, were also performed in England before the Protestant Reformation in the 1530s and 1540s.

From the sixteenth century in the Protestant churches of Europe, if music was allowed in worship at all, the emphasis was on hymn singing rather than chanting. The chorales that were sung in Lutheran and other churches stimulated the composition of an extensive repertoire of solo organ music. Before a congregation sang a hymn or a chorale, some or all of the tune was played by the organist so that the people knew what to sing. This playing of the tune was thus a prelude to the congregation's singing of it. Chorale preludes varied considerably in style, ranging from the simple and meditative to the grand and brilliant. They were usually written so as to reflect the sentiments of the original words to which the melody was sung. Thus a chorale prelude based on a Christmas tune would be bright and joyful; one based on a Passiontide hymn would be sombre and reflective. The organist would be expected to choose appropriate stops when playing these pieces.

There were also many sets of 'chorale variations' for organ. Here, the basic melody was in effect rewritten in different ways. These variations may well have originated from the practice of improvising or embellishing existing melodies. Certainly they allowed the organist to demonstrate the various stops and

J. S. Bach: Toccata from 'Toccata and Fugue in D minor'. This work is probably the best-known piece of organ music. The toccata is full of virtuoso writing for the hands and dramatic chords, as the opening few bars show. The speed, dynamic and registration markings are modern.

combinations of the instrument as well as the player's virtuosity. The term **partita** (probably from the French *partie*, denoting a piece in several parts or sections) was sometimes used as the title of a set of variations for organ or other keyboard instrument.

A **passacaglia** (probably from the Spanish dance *pasacalle*) is also a set of variations, with a short musical phrase being repeated over and over again throughout the piece. The composer then varies the accompaniment to this melody. Many organ passacaglias have the repeated melody as the pedal part, with the embellishments in the manual parts. A **chaconne** is similar in structure, except that a chord progression rather than a melody is used as the basis of the variations.

Not all organ music is based on existing melodies such as chorale tunes or plainchant. Much of it is 'free' composition with themes written by the composer as the basis of the pieces.

The **toccata** is usually a piece with fast-moving scale passages. The pedal part, where it is included, may also move rapidly, often as a solo, showing off the organist's virtuosity. The word comes from the Italian *toccare*, 'to touch', the implication being that the keys have to be touched lightly or quickly.

A toccata may be played on its own or it may be linked with a **fugue**. A fugue is

J. S. Bach: Fugue from 'Toccata and Fugue in D minor'. Fugues usually begin with the statement of the fugue theme, after which it is repeated in two or more other parts, with a countermelody or melodies played against it, as shown above. Finally, the fugue theme or subject appears in the pedals (below). The speed and dynamic markings are modern, as are the indications of which foot to use. A mark above the stave denotes use of the right foot, below the left. A 'u' denotes use of the heel, a '^' the toe.

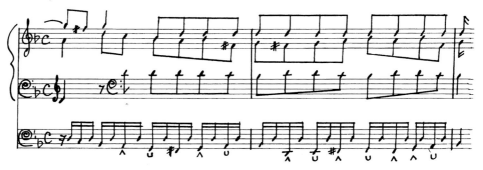

like a canon or a round, with the melody or theme being played on its own and then repeated against a countermelody until several musical parts are being played at the same time. A second melody may then appear in contrast to the first. This is also treated fugally. The first theme may then reappear in conjunction with the second one. In large organ fugues the themes and the counter melodies are played by both hands and feet.

Fugues may be linked with other pieces, such as a **fantasia** or a **prelude**. A prelude simply precedes the fugue and may be in a variety of musical styles. A fantasia is usually free-ranging in character, often sounding like a well-thought-out

Jan Sweelinck: 'Fantasia in Echo'. The organ is capable of sharp contrasts, especially loud stops on one manual and soft stops on another. This facility has been used to good effect by composers, as shown in this early example by Sweelinck.

improvisation rather than a fully composed piece of music. It may, for example, combine majestic chords with virtuoso scales and arpeggios for the hands and feet.

There are many other forms of organ music. The term **sonata** has a long history and denotes many different kinds of piece. The word literally means 'sound-piece' and originally described a musical composition consisting of one movement only. By the eighteenth century, however, sonatas could have as many as three movements. Organ sonatas were modelled on the instrumental trio sonatas, with their fast-slow-fast sections. By the beginning of the nineteenth century the sonata normally had four movements.

The term **voluntary** is peculiar to English organ music. It is thought to have originated as a freely composed or improvised piece of music played by the organist during the church service. Voluntaries vary considerably in style. They may be based on a hymn tune or other melody, and they can have one or more movements. Eighteenth-century voluntaries often have two movements, a slow 'Diapason' section, followed by a quicker one, using full organ or a solo stop (Cornet, Trumpet, Flute).

There are many **concertos** written for the organ. Usually the organ is accompanied by an orchestra, as with other concertos, though there are many solo passages for the organ during the composition. The organ concerto, like most concertos, usually has three movements.

Much other music has been arranged for the organ, especially when the organ was being used as a substitute for an orchestra. The **orchestral transcription** was especially popular in the nineteenth century, though adapting music originally written for other instruments is a tradition that dates back at least to the seventeenth century. In the Victorian period, excerpts from operas, symphonies and other instrumental and vocal pieces were all arranged for organ solo. It was not uncommon, when the town-hall or concert-hall organ was popular, for recitals to consist solely of transcriptions of such compositions as 'The Ride of the Valkyries' from Wagner's Ring cycle!

Composers

Only the major composers are mentioned here. The further reading section gives details of other books that include information about organ music and organ composers.

Johann Sebastian Bach (1685–1750) is often thought of as the first great composer of organ music. However, the organ had already been in existence for several hundred years before he was born and there were many fine organists and writers of organ music working in earlier centuries. Some of the earliest organ music was also designed to be played on other keyboard instruments – partly because an organ might not be available, partly because there was less of a distinction between different kinds of musical writing and partly because it would make the compositions more attractive to a larger number of potential players. English organ music, which was for manuals only until the early nineteenth century, was often labelled 'for organ or harpsichord' so that it would sell more easily. Some twentieth-century composers wrote their music for either organ or harmonium for similar reasons.

The best known early composers of keyboard and organ music include **Jan Sweelinck** (1562–1621), organist of the Oude Kerk, Amsterdam; **Jehan Titelouze** (1563–1633), organist of Rouen Cathedral; **Michael Praetorius** (1571–1621), German organist and writer on music and the organ; **Girolamo Frescobaldi** (1583–1643), organist of St Peter's Church, Rome; **Samuel Scheidt** (1587–1654), German organist and a pupil of Sweelinck; and **Johann Jakob Froberger** (1610–67), a Frenchman who worked in Austria and Italy and studied with Frescobaldi, as well as travelling elsewhere in Europe.

St Nicholas, Flensburg, Germany. Organ by N. Maas, 1604–8. The two angels at the top of the case originally sounded actual trumpet pipes! The Hauptwerk was the main division, with only four stops on the Brustwerk beneath. Note the twin Rückpositiv cases.

Nieuwe Kerk, Amsterdam, Holland. A typically opulent seventeenth-century Dutch civic organ.

Works by these organ composers are still played regularly and form a major part of the repertoire. Each composer contributed to the development of one or more of the musical forms described earlier in this chapter. Sweelinck, for instance, is remembered for his fantasias (including the 'Echo' Fantasia, which uses loud and soft stops on different manuals to produce echoes), toccatas and variations. His best known work is probably the Variations on the popular song 'Mein junges Leben hat ein End' ('My young life hath an end'). This is a series of embellishments on the same melody, beginning and ending with simple variations, with more complex and virtuosic variations in between. Music such as this was probably written to be played during 'promenade' concerts in the church and not for purposes of church worship.

Frescobaldi's music for the Catholic Church would be played before, during or after the service. He was famous, like Sweelinck, for his virtuoso and expressive playing and is particularly remembered for his toccatas. Titelouze wrote many organ hymns and magnificats (pieces based on the magnificat plainsong melodies). Praetorius composed in a wide range of styles and forms, as did Scheidt and Froberger.

English organ composers during the sixteenth and seventeenth centuries composed for smaller instruments, which were unlikely to have had pedals, and so the music could also be performed on other keyboard instruments. One of the most famous keyboard composers of his day was **John Bull** (1562–1628). After a period as organist of Hereford Cathedral and the Chapel Royal, London, he moved to Brussels as organist of the Royal Chapel and then to Antwerp, where he became organist at the cathedral. He was a close friend of Sweelinck and the two men obviously influenced each other in their compositions.

Sweelinck was a major influence on the development of organ playing and organ composition, having a number of pupils who became famous players and composers in their own right. By the end of the seventeenth century, just as individual styles or schools of organ building were emerging, so groups of organ composers, with different approaches and styles, were developing in each major country.

As the most highly developed instruments were built in Germany and Scandinavia, so the major school of organ composition, which still forms the basis of the organist's repertoire, developed in these areas. **Dietrich Buxtehude** (1637–1707) was of Danish origin, though he spent most of his working life as organist in Lübeck, Germany. He wrote much orchestral and choral music as well as an extensive range of compositions for the organ consisting of toccatas, preludes, fantasias and fugues, chaconnes and a large number of chorale preludes.

Johann Sebastian Bach (1685–1750) greatly admired Buxtehude's playing and music and walked many miles from his home to Lübeck to hear him. Bach might have succeeded Buxtehude as organist there, but he was not successful in the final competition for the post. It is said that he would have had to marry Buxtehude's daughter as part of the contract!

Bach's life was spent as organist, music director and composer to a number of churches and ducal courts in Germany. From 1723 until his death he was Kantor at St Thomas's Church, Leipzig, where much of his church music was composed. He came from a large musical family and was part of the German organist-composer tradition. He had over twenty children, many of whom were fine musicians and composers in their own right. Bach is regarded as the greatest composer of organ music and one of the greatest composers of any music of any period.

Over two hundred organ compositions written in a wide variety of styles form the backbone of the organist's repertoire. Bach wrote the best-known organ piece of all, the Toccata and Fugue in D minor. It is generally regarded as an early work, though with its dramatic opening and sharp contrasts, its virtuoso fugue and final climax it is easy to understand why it has always been popular. This piece is one of a group of large-scale compositions that link an introductory toccata, fantasia, prelude or similar movement with a substantial fugue.

The chorale preludes and pieces based on hymn tunes are more reflective in style. The *Orgelbüchlein* ('Little Organ Book'), though not completed, contains chorale preludes for all parts of the church's year. Some of the other chorale preludes are less well known, though equally magnificent; the *Clavierübung* Part III is a collection of chorale preludes and settings of parts of the plainsong mass with a great Prelude at the start and the well-known 'St Anne' Fugue (so called because the fugue melody is like the opening of the hymn tune 'St Anne' – 'O God our help in ages past') at the end. *Clavierübung* means literally 'keyboard practice' and the other parts of this great anthology contain music for harpsichord or other instruments. Part III is devoted almost entirely to organ music and the technique of the organist is certainly tested in playing these pieces. The six Schübler Chorale Preludes are named after their publisher and are mainly arrangements for organ of movements from Bach's choral cantatas, including the well-known movement from 'Wachet auf, ruft uns die Stimme!' Bach was an avid student of music other than

St Laurents, Rotterdam, Holland. A typical late-twentieth-century baroque organ, with four manuals, built by Marcussen of Denmark in 1973.

his own and he arranged (and often improved) compositions and based some of his works on their themes. A number of Antonio Vivaldi's string concertos survive in arrangements by Bach for organ.

As Bach was an organ teacher, some of his organ music, for example the *Clavierübung,* was at least partly written as 'practice music' for his pupils. The trio sonatas, too, were designed to develop the player's independence of hands and feet. Some of the music was probably played on a pedal harpsichord as well as or instead of an organ and is chamber rather than church music. When organs were hand-blown it would be much easier and more comfortable to practise at home on a harpsichord!

Many of Bach's contemporaries also wrote music that is still played. **Johann Pachelbel** (1653–1706) held a number of important posts including that of organist of St Stephen's Cathedral in Vienna. **Vincent Lübeck** (1654–1706), **Georg Böhm** (1661–1733), **Nikolaus Bruhns** (1665–97), **Johann Gottfried Walther** (1684–1748) and **Johann Ludwig Krebs** (1713–80) all composed organ music that is familiar today.

Very different traditions of organ composition were developing in France and England during the eighteenth century. The French organ relied less on the pedals and more on the reed stops. The stop registration became very stylised – if not standardised – and the music reflects this. The organ mass was linked directly to the use of the instrument in the liturgy. More frivolous pieces, based on dance movements for example, were also composed, though these would be played on chamber rather than church organs. The main composers in a strong native tradition were **François Couperin** (1668–1733), organist to the king and one of a family of musicians; **Nicolas de Grigny** (1671–1703), of Rheims; **Louis Nicolas Clérambault** (1676–1738), of Paris; and **Jean François d'Andrieu** (1682–1738), also of Paris. Many of their pieces were published in anthologies, such as Clérambault's *Livre d'Orgue* and d'Andrieu's *Pièces d'Orgue*. Couperin wrote and published two large-scale organ masses, one for parish churches (*Messe pour les Paroisses*) and one for monasteries (*Messe pour les Convents*). Couperin corresponded extensively with Bach, some of whose music was undoubtedly influenced by the French composer; in particular, some of the rhythms used in French organ music (such as the *notes inégales*) are also found in Bach's pieces, as, for example, the great Prelude in E flat that opens the *Clavierübung*.

There was less interest in organ composition in England than on the continent. After the Restoration of the Monarchy in 1660 organists were again appointed to church and cathedral posts and some organ music was composed. **John Blow** (1649–1708) and his pupil **Henry Purcell** (1659–95) were both in their turn organist of Westminster Abbey and composers of much organ music, especially voluntaries. Purcell's most famous organ piece is probably the Voluntary on the 'Old Hundredth' hymn tune. The major English organists of the eighteenth century all composed organ music, including: **William Croft** (1678–1727), also for a time organist of Westminster Abbey; **Maurice Greene** (1695–1755), organist of St Paul's Cathedral; **William Boyce** (1710–79), Master of the King's Music; **William Walond** (1725–70) of Oxford; and **John Stanley** (1713–86). Stanley was the most prolific and best known, and several sets of voluntaries were

John Stanley: 'Voluntary in D minor'. English eighteenth-century organ music was much simpler than, for example, German music of the period. There was no pedal part, and the music relied on solo stops and contrasts between loud and soft manuals for the main effects, as in this voluntary.

St Lawrence, Whitchurch, Little Stanmore, Middlesex. The new organ by Goetze & Gwynn made in 1994 incorporated the surviving parts of Gerard Smith's instrument of 1716. Handel played this organ when he worked for the Duke of Chandos at Canons in 1717 and 1718.

published in his lifetime. Although blind, he was organist of the Temple Church in London, where he played the fine Bernard Smith organ. Handel is reputed to have rushed to hear Stanley play his final voluntaries, so highly did he regard his playing.

George Frideric Handel (1685–1759) composed little organ music. The bulk of his output for the organ takes the form of concertos for organ and orchestra that were designed to be played as interludes between acts of his operas or oratorios.

Small organs were installed in theatres and opera houses for this purpose. There were even pipe organs in the London pleasure gardens (such as Vauxhall) for the playing of organ concertos. Many of these pieces were composed in such a hurry that Handel had time only to write out the orchestral parts, improvising the organ solos as he went along. Even today, many printed versions of the concertos have the instruction *Organo ad libitum* and nothing more in the score.

By the end of the eighteenth century the organ was not as favoured an instrument as it had been. The orchestra was increasingly popular and, as the piano developed as a powerful and expressive solo instrument, fewer composers of the first rank were attracted to the organ. **Wolfgang Amadeus Mozart** (1756–91) wrote some music, ostensibly for musical clock with organ pipes, that may be played on larger church instruments. **Franz Joseph Haydn** (1732–1809) wrote only small-scale organ works, as did **Ludwig van Beethoven** (1770–1827).

In the nineteenth century much organ music was transcribed from orchestral or choral music. Among the few notable composers who wrote for the organ, **Felix Mendelssohn** (1809–47) composed six sonatas – all substantial works – as well as three preludes and fugues and a number of other small-scale pieces. Like many organ composers before and since, he was a virtuoso player and gave many recitals.

Pécs Cathedral, Hungary. A modern console, with registration aids controlled from a computer inside the console.

Some celebrated virtuosos composed a small number of pieces for the organ. **Franz Liszt** (1811–86), the great Hungarian piano virtuoso, wrote mammoth compositions for the organ which demonstrated both the player's virtuosity and the power and dynamic range of the large organs on which the pieces were initially played. The most famous of these compositions is arguably the Fantasia and Fugue on BACH (the note B in Germany is actually B flat; the note H is B natural). With its virtuoso keyboard writing, the piece taxes the technique of any player!

Julius Reubke (1834–58) looked set to emulate Liszt with his massive Sonata on the 94th Psalm. He died young and this piece was his only major composition, though it remains a significant contribution to the repertoire.

Robert Schumann (1810–56) also wrote six fugues on the name of Bach as well as four sketches for pedal piano (a piano whose lower notes were activated also by an organ pedalboard – a useful practice instrument, like the pedal harpsichord). **Johannes Brahms** (1833–97) also wrote organ pieces, including thirteen delightful miniatures based on chorale tunes. Probably the best known is 'Es ist ein Ros' entsprungen' ('A beautiful rose has blossomed').

Franz Liszt: 'Fantasia and Fugue on BACH'. Nineteenth-century organ music required larger, more powerful instruments that could give a broad range of dynamics and timbres. The end of this virtuoso piece by Liszt shows the extremes needed, all within the space of ten bars. The music is much more chordal than contrapuntal and employs rapid harmonic changes, such as the change from G flat major to B major in the space of the first three bars of the example.

Johannes Brahms: 'Es ist ein Ros' entsprungen'. Some nineteenth-century organ music was modelled on the earlier chorale prelude, as in this short and simple example by Brahms. The music is chordal, like some of Bach's simpler preludes, and the melody is in the upper part of the right hand, where it is embellished.

The most prolific German organ composers, all themselves regular players, were **Josef Rheinberger** (1840–1901), **Max Reger** (1873–1916) and **Sigfrid Karg-Elert** (1877–1935). Rheinberger is chiefly remembered for his twenty organ sonatas, which are now enjoying a revival in popularity. Reger was a prolific composer of all kinds of music and his organ repertoire is varied, including preludes, fantasias, toccatas and fugues as well as much chorale-based writing. It is notable for its complexity, being written for the heavy German organs of the late nineteenth and early twentieth centuries. Karg-Elert based much of his music on chorales, and his *Improvisations* are still popular in the repertoire.

As a result of the Cavaillé-Coll organ and the work of organ tutors at the Paris Conservatoire, a substantial school of organ composition developed in France in the nineteenth century and continued in the twentieth. Though his own output was small, **César Franck** (1822–90) had a significant influence on French organists and organ composers through his distinctive style, as evinced by the *Six Pieces* and the *Three Chorals*, his last work. **Charles-Marie Widor** (1845–1937), famous for the toccata from his Fifth Organ Symphony, wrote much organ music, including nine organ symphonies.

Much exciting and often difficult music has been written for the organ by French composers. Organists writing in the twentieth century included **Jean Langlais**, **Charles Tournemire**, **Joseph Jongen**, **Jehan Alain** and **Olivier Messiaen**. Tournemire wrote some fifty-one organ masses. Alain was killed while still young, but his well-known piece *Litanies* shows what a great composer he would have been. Messiaen was perhaps the greatest organ composer of the twentieth century. His organ pieces indicate his highly religious background combined with an interest in bird song and non-western tonalities and a highly individual rhythmic structure.

St Mary, Bathwick, Bath. A three-manual organ by Gray, now in the Musical Instrument Museum in Berlin. Note the large stopknobs, the straight jambs on which they are set and the distance between the keyboards. As the more orchestral styles of playing developed, jambs were angled and stops made smaller in order to ease the task of changing registration, along with thumb and toe pistons. Keyboards were brought closer together so that manuals could be changed easily.

Many of his compositions centre upon the church's calendar and scenes from the life of Christ, for example, *La Nativité* and *L'Ascension*.

No other European school of organ composition compares with that in France in the late nineteenth and twentieth centuries. Most of the great twentieth-century composers such as Britten, Tippett, Stravinsky and Shostakovich either did not write music for the organ or produced only a handful of compositions. Other famous composers have begun their careers as organists and church musicians but have left little organ music. Edward Elgar is a good example. Though a church organist, he composed only one piece for the organ, the *Sonata* in G. There are many organ composers from England, Germany, Scandinavia and, increasingly, North America, but none has yet achieved the stature of either Messiaen or the great writers of organ music of earlier centuries.

There is a rich catalogue of music for the instrument that can regularly be heard in churches and concert halls, at services, recitals and concerts. Though the organ is primarily a solo or an accompanimental instrument, there are also concertos by composers of every age that are frequently played. At the highest professional levels of organ playing, standards of performance have never been better, as a result of the thorough training available at colleges and universities in Britain, Europe and North America. While there is a shortage of people willing to play the church organ in many places, competition for organ scholarships and concert engagements is fierce. Being an organist – at whatever level of competence – is not easy and the organ student must devote many hours to practice and study of the instrument and its construction. Once mastered, however, the organ is rewarding to play. It is equally satisfying to listen to good organs and well-played organ music. Modern recording techniques have ensured that high-quality performances on historic organs from

St Mary the Great, Cambridge. Organ originally by 'Father' Smith, 1698. The four-tower and three-flat case arrangement became popular in the eighteenth century.

St Endellion, Cornwall. New organ by Goetze & Gwynn, based on the organ of St Mary, Finedon, Northamptonshire.

St Botolph, Aldersgate. Case of organ by Samuel Green, 1791. Note the 'Regency' style.

many countries are readily available to anyone interested in the instrument and its music.

No other instrument has the same dynamic range, the same multiplicity of colours, the same rich and varied heritage as the organ. No other instrument stretches the mind and body of the player in the way that the organ does. It is a unique instrument, which continues to fascinate and excite many people, whether as players or listeners. It is truly the King of Instruments.

Above left: *The organ of Gibraltar Cathedral. A nineteenth-century organ, with a new Chair case by Richard Bower.*

Above right: *St Michael and All Angels, SouthWestoe, South Shields, County Durham. New organ by Goetze & Gwynn, based on eighteenth-century English models.*

The organ of Pembroke College, Cambridge; a two-manual organ built by Noel Mander in 1980, based on early-eighteenth-century pipework and case.

4
Gazetteer

This gazetteer lists a number of organs in the United Kingdom that are worth visiting, because they are of historic importance, are major examples of individual builders' work, or represent the best of a particular style of organ building. For further details, check the *National Pipe Organ Register* (http://lehuray2.csi.cam.ac.uk/npor.html) run by the British Institute of Organ Studies (BIOS).

Appleby, Cumbria: St Lawrence. Seventeenth-century case and some pipes moved from Carlisle Cathedral in 1684.

Armitage, Staffordshire: Parish Church. Case and some pipes from the 1790 organ by Samuel Green, originally built for Lichfield Cathedral.

Ashridge, Hertfordshire: Management College. Two-manual organ by Thomas Elliot, 1818.

Bath, Somerset: Abbey. Four-manual organ originally built by William Hill, 1868. Rebuilt Klais, 1997.

Belfast, Northern Ireland: Ulster Hall. Four-manual organ by William Hill, 1861, 1903. Restored and enlarged by Mander, 1978, 1982. Widely regarded as one of Hill's finest instruments.

Beverley, East Yorkshire: Minster. Large four-manual organ by Hill, 1884, 1916, incorporating much of the original pipework from the Snetzler organ of 1769.

Bexleyheath, Kent: Hall Place. Chamber organ by George England, 1760. Bourne Road, London, DA5 1 PQ. Telephone: 01322 526574. Website: www.hallplace.com.

Birmingham: Cathedral. Case by Thomas Schwarbrick, 1715.

Birmingham: Symphony Hall. Large four-manual concert organ by Klais, 2001.

Birmingham: Town Hall. Four-manual organ by Mander, 1984 and 2007, based on the William Hill organ of 1834, with additions in 1843, 1890 and 1933.

Blackburn, Lancashire: Cathedral. Large four-manual organ by J. W. Walker, 1969, in open, caseless position; enlarged Wood, 2002.

Blair Atholl, Perth and Kinross: Blair Castle, Blair Atholl, Pitlochry PH18 5TL. Telephone: 01796 481207. Website: www.blair-castle.co.uk. Positive-regal by John Loosemore, 1650.

Blandford Forum, Dorset: St Peter and St Paul. Three-manual organ by George Pike England, 1794; rebuilt Hill, 1876; restored Mander, 1971.

Brentford, Middlesex: The Musical Museum, 399 High Street, Brentford, Middlesex TW8 0DU. Telephone: 020 8560 8108. Website: www.musicalmuseum.co.uk. Includes a Wurlitzer organ originally built for the Regal Theatre, Kingston upon Thames.

Bressingham, Norfolk: St John the Baptist's Church. Barrel organ thought to be by Flight, 1859.

Bristol: Anglican Cathedral. Four-manual organ originally built by Renatus Harris, 1685; rebuilt by J. W. Walker, 1907. Restored Mander, 1989/90. Harris's original main case survives, though somewhat altered.

Bristol: Colston Hall. Large four-manual concert-hall organ by Harrison & Harrison, 1956.

Bristol: Roman Catholic Cathedral. Modern three-manual classical organ built by Rieger of Austria, 1973.

Bristol: St Mary Redcliffe Church. Large four-manual organ by Harrison & Harrison, originally built 1912 and widely regarded as amongst the firm's finest instruments.

Bury St Edmunds, Suffolk: Moyse's Hall Museum, Cornhill, Bury St Edmunds IP33 1DZ.

Telephone: 01284 706183. Website: www.stedmundsbury.gov.uk/moysmain.htm. Includes a chamber organ.

Cambridge: Christ's College. Early-eighteenth-century organ case and some pipes, possibly built by Bernard Smith; restored 1983.

Cambridge: Emmanuel College. Three-manual organ by Kenneth Jones, using casework from *c*.1686.

Cambridge: Jesus College. Small organ by Bishop, 1849, based on Bernard Smith pipes and restored by Mander, 1970. Large organ by Kuhn, 2007.

Cambridge: King's College. Main case by Dallam, 1606; Chair case by Pease, 1661. Four-manual organ by Harrison & Harrison, 1934; revised 1968.

Cambridge: Pembroke College. Two-manual organ consisting of Great, Chair and Pedal, built by Mander in 1980 and based on early-eighteenth-century pipework and case.

Cambridge: Peterhouse. Three-manual Snetzler organ and case, 1765; restored and rebuilt, Mander, 1964.

Cambridge: St John's College. Large four-manual organ by Mander, 1994. Includes a famous *en chamade* Trumpet stop.

Cambridge: St Mary the Great (University Church). Largely original Bernard Smith three-manual organ and case, 1698; rebuilt 1870; restored 1963 and 1995. Parish organ by Kenneth Jones, 1991.

Cambridge: Trinity College. Three-manual organ by Metzler of Zürich, 1975, using main and Chair cases of the Bernard Smith organ of 1708, together with a few original pipes.

Canterbury, Kent: Cathedral. Three-manual 'Father' Willis, 1886; rebuilt Mander, 1979–80. This was one of Willis's first instruments to use electro-pneumatic action. The instrument now includes a 'nave' section.

Cardiff: Llandaff Cathedral. Complete new organ by Nicholson scheduled for completion by Easter, 2010.

Carisbrooke, Isle of Wight: Carisbrooke Castle Museum, Carisbrooke, Newport PO30 1XY. Telephone: 01983 523112. Website: www.carisbrookecastlemuseum.org.uk. Three-stop chamber organ built by Hoffheimer, *c*.1602. Thought to be of Flemish origin and built for John Graham, Earl of Montrose. Played by Princess Elizabeth, daughter of Charles I, while in captivity at Carisbrooke.

Cheltenham, Gloucestershire: Cheltenham Art Gallery and Museum, Clarence Street, Cheltenham GL50 3JT. Telephone: 01242 237431. Website: www.cheltenhammuseum.org.uk. Musical-instrument collection includes two small organs.

Chester, Cheshire: Cathedral. Large four-manual organ by Whiteley, 1876; Hill, 1910; conservatively rebuilt, 1969.

Chichester, West Sussex: Cathedral. Organ largely by William Hill, 1851, 1859 and 1888, but based on earlier work by Harris, 1678, and Byfield, 1725, and restored by Noel Mander in 1985. Includes a 'nave' section.

Christchurch, Dorset: Christchurch Priory. Large four-manual organ by Nicholson, 1999, incorporating parts of earlier instruments by Cumming (eighteenth-century) and 'Father' Willis. The organ has a 'nave' section and two four-manual consoles, one detached, with an electro-pneumatic system, the other a mainly mechanical action.

Cotton, Suffolk: Mechanical Music Museum and Bygones, Blacksmith's Road, Cotton, Stowmarket IP14 4QN. Telephone: 01449 613876. Website: www.cottonmusic.co.uk. Includes a large Mortier café organ and a Wurlitzer theatre organ originally in Leicester Square Theatre, London.

Coventry: Cathedral. Modern four-manual organ similar in design to the organ of the Royal Festival Hall, London, by Harrison & Harrison, 1962.

Crick, Northamptonshire: St Margaret of Antioch's Church. Three-manual organ by

Eton College, Lower Chapel. New organ by Kenneth Tickell, 2000, using French stop names. The case is modelled on those by 'Father' Smith, as for example at St Mary the Great, Cambridge.

Thomas Elliot, 1819, originally built for St James's Chapel Royal, London.

Doncaster, South Yorkshire: Parish Church. Five-manual organ by Schulze, 1862; rebuilt J. W. Walker, 1935; restored 1999 with new console by Nicholson.

Douglas, Isle of Man: Manx Museum and National Trust, Douglas IM1 3LY. Telephone: 01624 648001. Website: www.gov.im/tourism. Collection includes two barrel organs.

Downpatrick, Northern Ireland: Down Cathedral. Eighteenth-century case and possibly pipework; restored with additions by the Wells-Kennedy Partnership, 1989.

Downside Abbey, Stratton-on-the-Fosse, Somerset. 142-stop extension organ by Compton, 1937.

Dundee: Caird Hall. Three-manual organ by Harrison & Harrison, 1923, restored 1992. Designed by the blind organist Alfred Hollins.

Durham: Cathedral. Large four-manual organ by Harrison & Harrison, 1905, 1935, 1970, incorporating pipework by Willis. Parts of the case of the original Bernard Smith organ of 1683–4 survive.

East Bradenham, Norfolk: St Mary's Church. One-manual organ by Samuel Green, 1786.

Easton-on-the-Hill, Northamptonshire: All Saints' Church. Two-manual organ by Holdich, 1850. Includes a 'dumb organist' barrel attachment.

Edinburgh: Russell Collection of Harpsichords and Clavichords, St Cecilia's Hall, Niddry Street, Cowgate, Edinburgh EH1 1LJ. Telephone: 0131 650 2805. Website: www.music.ed.ac.uk/russell. Collection includes several small organs.

Edinburgh: University, Reid Concert Hall. Two-manual Werkprinzip organ by Ahrend of Denmark, 1978.

Ellesmere, Shropshire: Ellesmere College Great Hall. Three-manual organ by Schulze, originally built for St Mary's Church, Tyne Dock, 1864, 1874.

Ely, Cambridgeshire: Cathedral. Large four-manual Harrison & Harrison organ, 1908; rebuilt 1975; renovated, 2001. Widely regarded as the definitive Harrison organ. Case by Gilbert Scott, 1851, based on medieval Gothic examples.

Eton, Berkshire: Eton College. The Chapel contains a large four-manual organ by Hill, 1882, 1902, rebuilt with tubular-pneumatic action by Mander. The Memorial Hall contains main and Chair cases and some pipes from the Mittenreiter organ built in 1773 for the English Church in Rotterdam, rebuilt in 1975 by Flentrop of Zaandam, Holland. The Lower Chapel has a three-manual organ by Kenneth Tickell.

Eton College Chapel. Four-manual organ by Hill, 1882 and 1902. Rebuilt by N. P. Mander with tubular-pneumatic action.

Everingham, East Yorkshire: St Mary and St Everilda's Church. Two-manual organ by Charles Allen, 1837/9; restored 1988/9 by Mander. Organ tuned to unequal temperament.

Exeter, Devon: Cathedral. Great and Chair cases of John Loosemore organ of 1665. Present instrument by Willis, 1891; Harrison & Harrison, 1936, 1965, 2003.

Farnborough, Hampshire: St Michael's Abbey. Two-manual organ by the Cavaillé-Coll company, 1905.

Finedon, Northamptonshire: St Mary's Church. Three-manual organ reputedly by Christopher Shrider, 1717, largely unaltered. Shrider was Bernard Smith's son-in-law. It is now thought that the organ may have been by Smith himself. The instrument was conservatively rebuilt in the nineteenth century by Holdich.

Framingham Pigot, Norfolk: St Andrew's Church. Organ by Holdich, 1860. Includes an example of his Diaocton stop – an octave coupler with additional octaves of pipes to the ranks affected.

Framlingham, Suffolk: St Michael's Church. Organ by Thomas Thamar, 1674, originally built for Pembroke College, Cambridge. The case is reputed to be older still.

Glasgow: Glasgow Art Gallery and Museum, Kelvingrove, Glasgow G3 8AG. Telephone: 0141 276 9599. Website: www.clyde-valley.com/glasgow/kelvingr.htm. Three-manual organ by Lewis, 1901. Restored 1989 by Mander.

Gloucester: Cathedral. Four-manual organ by Hill, Norman & Beard, 1971, incorporating pipes from the original Harris organ of 1665 and the original main and Chair cases. Rebuilt and enlarged by Nicholson, 1999-2003.

Gooderstone, Norfolk: St George's Church. Chamber organ possibly by Bishop, *c*.1820. Includes a very early example of composition pedals.

Goudhurst, Kent: Finchcocks Living Museum of Music, Goudhurst TN17 1HH. Telephone: 01580 211702. Website: www.finchcocks.co.uk. Includes several chamber and barrel organs, including a fine instrument of 1766 by John Byfield II.

Gravesend, Kent: St George's Church. Includes much material from the organ by George England, 1764.

Great Budworth, Cheshire: St Mary and All Saints. Two-manual organ by Samuel Renn, 1839. Restored by Goetze and Gwynn, 2004.

Great Packington, Warwickshire: St James's Church. Organ by Thomas Parker (originally thought to be by Richard Bridge), designed by Handel, 1749. Enlarged by Snetzler, 1760. The organ was originally built for Charles Jennens, the librettist of *Messiah*.

Halifax, West Yorkshire: Parish Church. Four-manual Harrison & Harrison organ, 1929, incorporating some pipes from the Snetzler organ of 1766.

Hexham, Northumberland: Abbey. Large two-manual organ by Lawrence Phelps, modelled on the French classical organ.

Hillington, Norfolk: St Mary the Virgin's Church. Two-manual chamber organ by Snetzler, 1756.

Hillsborough, Northern Ireland: Parish Church. Case and much pipework by Snetzler, 1773. There is also a one-manual organ by G. P. England, 1795.

Horsham, West Sussex: Christ's Hospital Chapel. Large organ by Rushworth & Dreaper, 1931, 1981.

Huddersfield, West Yorkshire: St Paul's Hall, University of Huddersfield. Three-manual Werkprinzip organ by Wood of Huddersfield, 1977; restored 1997.

Huddersfield, West Yorkshire: Town Hall. Four-manual organ by Willis, 1880, restored Harrison & Harrison, 1980.

Hull, East Yorkshire: City Hall. Large four-manual organ by Compton, 1950, based on the Forster & Andrews instrument of 1911; restored 1985/91.

Hull, East Yorkshire: Holy Trinity Church. Large four-manual organ by Compton, 1939, based on the Forster & Andrews instrument of 1876, 1908.

A series of chest and chamber organs; top two and centre left, built by N. P. Mander Ltd; centre right, built for Pluscarden Abbey, Elgin, Moray, Scotland, by Kenneth Tickell & Co; bottom two by Goetze & Gwynn.

Kidderminster, Worcestershire: Town Hall. Three-manual organ by Hill, 1854.

Kilmarnock, East Ayrshire: Dean Castle, Dean Road, Kilmarnock KA3 1XB. Telephone: 01563 522702 or 574916. Website: www.deancastle.com. Musical instrument collection includes several early small organs.

King's Lynn, Norfolk: St Margaret's Church. The case and some pipes (including the first manual double known in an English instrument) from Snetzler's large three-manual organ of 1754 remain.

Leeds, West Yorkshire: Parish Church. Large four-manual organ in Victorian Gothic case with no pipes.

Leeds, West Yorkshire: St Bartholomew's Church, Armley. Four-manual organ by Schulze, 1869.

Leeds, West Yorkshire: Town Hall. Three-manual organ by Wood, Wordsworth of Leeds, 1972, based on a five-manual instrument by Gray & Davison, 1859, 1865.

Leicester: Cathedral. Four-manual organ by Harrison & Harrison, 1930, incorporating pipework from the Snetzler organ of 1774; altered 1972/3 and 1983.

Lichfield, Staffordshire: Cathedral. Four-manual organ by Hill, 1884, 1908, but based on an instrument built in 1860 by G. M. Holdich; rebuilt 1973 by Hill, Norman & Beard and restored and enlarged 2000 by Harrison & Harrison, when a 'nave' organ was added. At the time it was first constructed by Holdich, this organ had one of the most complete Pedal divisions of any cathedral organ in Britain.

Lincoln: Cathedral. Last cathedral organ built by 'Father' Willis, 1898. Conservatively rebuilt and restored, 1960, by Harrison & Harrison and again in 1998.

Liskeard, Cornwall: Paul Corin's Magnificent Music Machines, St Keyne Station, Liskeard PL14 4SH. Telephone: 01579 343108. Website: www.paulcorinmusic.co.uk. The collection includes several mechanical organs and the 1929 Wurlitzer organ previously in the Regent Theatre, Brighton.

Little Bardfield, Essex: St Katherine's Church. Organ originally built for Jesus College, Cambridge, with case by Renatus Harris, 1680.

Little Walsingham, Norfolk: St Mary's Church. Two-manual organ by Cedric Arnold Williamson & Hyatt, 1964. An early British classical organ.

Liverpool: Anglican Cathedral. Five-manual organ by Willis, 1923–6, 1960–5; rebuilt Harrison & Harrison, 1977; a high-pressure Trompette Militaire was added in the Corona, 1998 and a central division in 2007. The largest pipe organ in Britain. There is also a two-manual organ in the Cathedral's Lady Chapel.

Liverpool: Liverpool Museum, William Brown Street, Liverpool L3 8EN. Telephone: 0151 478 4392. Website: www.liverpoolmuseums.org.uk. Includes a portative organ by Nicolaus Wandersheid, Nuremberg, 1644, a 1767 Snetzler chamber organ, a 'bottle' organ and a barrel organ.

Liverpool: Roman Catholic Cathedral. Large four-manual organ by J. W. Walker, 1967.

Liverpool: St George's Hall, L1 1JJ. Telephone: 0151 225 6909. Website: www.stgeorgesliverpool.co.uk. Large four-manual concert organ by Willis, 1854–5, 1897, 1931.

London: The British Museum, Great Russell Street, London WC1B 3DG. Telephone: 020 7323 8990. Website: www.thebritishmuseum.org. The musical instrument collections contain early Pan-pipes.

London: Buckingham Palace, Ballroom. Telephone: 020 7930 4832. Website: www.royal.gov.uk. Organ by H. C. Lincoln originally built for the Royal Pavilion, Brighton; restored William Drake, 2002. The private chapel had an organ by Samuel Green, 1790, now in Kensington Palace.

London: Christ Church, Spitalfields. Large three-manual organ and case by Richard Bridge, 1735. Largely unaltered, though not currently playable.

London: The Iveagh Bequest, Kenwood, Hampstead Lane, London NW3 7JR. Telephone: 020 8348 1286. Includes a chamber organ by John England, c.1790.

London: Mander Organs Limited, Tower Hamlets, St Peter's Organ Works, St Peter's Square, London E2 7AF. Telephone: 020 7739 4747. Website: www.mander-organs.com. A small collection of chamber and table organs.

London: Regent's Park. St Katherine's Church. Organ by Samuel Green, 1778; restored Mander, 1998.

London: Royal Albert Hall, Kensington SW7 2AP. Telephone: 0845 401 5045. Website: www.royalalberthall.com. Large four-manual organ by Harrison & Harrison, 1926, based on the 1871 organ by 'Father' Willis; restored Mander, 2003/4.

London: Royal College of Music Museum of Instruments, Prince Consort Road, South Kensington, London SW7 2BS. Telephone: 020 7589 3643. Website: www.cph.rcm.ac.uk. Collection includes a table regal, c.1629, and a chamber organ possibly by Bernard Smith, 1702.

London: Royal Festival Hall, Belvedere Road, South Bank SE1 8XX. Telephone: 0207 928 2228. Website: www.southbankcentre.co.uk. Caseless four-manual organ by Harrison & Harrison, 1954. The first large British organ to return to a classical specification and methods of voicing.

London: Royal Naval College, Greenwich. Telephone: 020 8269 4715. Website: www.oldroyalnavalcollege.org. Three-manual organ and case originally by Samuel Green, 1789.

London: St Andrew by the Wardrobe. Chamber organ by Snetzler, originally built for Teddesley Hall, Staffordshire, 1769.

London: St Anne, Limehouse. Three-manual organ built originally for the Great Exhibition of 1851 by Gray & Davison; restored by William Drake, 2006.

London: St Botolph, Aldgate. Three-manual organ by Goetze and Gwynn, based on the case and pipes of a Renatus Harris instrument of the 1670s, rebuilt by John Byfield in 1744.

London: St Bride, Fleet Street. Large four-manual extension organ by Compton, 1958; restored 2002.

London: St Giles, Camberwell. Large, almost untouched three-manual organ by Bishop, 1844; restored 1961.

London: St Giles, Cripplegate. Three-manual organ by Mander based on a case and pipes by Jordan & Bridge, 1733. Two-manual organs by Mander and Tickell, 2008.

London: St James, Bermondsey. Three-manual organ by Bishop, 1829; restored by Goetze and Gwynn, 2002.

London: St James, Clerkenwell. Two-manual organ and case by George Pike England, 1792; restored by Mander, 1978.

London: St Leonard, Shoreditch. Organ case by Bridge, 1756.

London: St Magnus the Martyr, London Bridge. Case of 1712 organ by Abraham Jordan, reputed to contain the first swell box in Britain.

London: St Mary, Rotherhithe. Three-manual organ by Byfield, 1764, largely unaltered; restored Mander, 1959; Goetze & Gwynn, 1991.

London: St Mary-at-Hill. Two/three-manual organ by William Hill, 1848, 1879, largely unaltered, restored after fire damage by Mander, 2000/2.

London: St Mary Magdalene, Holloway Road. Organ by George Pike England, 1814, rebuilt by 'Father' Willis in 1867. Willis was organist of the church for over thirty years.

London: St Paul's Cathedral. Five-manual organ by Mander, 1977, refurbished 2007/8, based on the 'Father' Willis organ of 1872. Cases from the original Bernard Smith organ of 1697, designed by Sir Christopher Wren. Includes a 'nave' section.

London: St Peter, Cornhill. Three-manual organ with case and some pipes by Bernard Smith, 1681.

London: St Vedast, Foster Lane. Three-manual organ originally built by Harris & Byfield.

London: Southwark Cathedral. Four-manual organ originally built by Lewis, 1896;

restored Harrison & Harrison, 1986.

London: Temple Church. Large four-manual Harrison & Harrison, 1927/54, originally built for the ballroom of Glentanar Castle, Scotland.

London: Victoria and Albert Museum, Cromwell Road, South Kensington, London SW7 2RL. Telephone: 020 7942 2000. Website: www.vam.ac.uk. Includes a combined harpsichord and organ of 1579.

London: Westminster Abbey. Five-manual organ by Harrison & Harrison, originally built 1937; rebuilt and enlarged by Harrison, 1982–7. Cases by J. L. Pearson, 1899.

London: Westminster Roman Catholic Cathedral. Large four-manual organ by Willis, 1922–32; restored Harrison & Harrison, 1984.

Lound, Suffolk. Two-manual organ by Harrison & Harrison, 1913, in a case by Comper.

Ludlow, Shropshire: Parish Church. Case and some pipes from the original Snetzler organ of 1764; restored Nicholson, 1982–8, 1999, 2006.

Lulworth, Dorset: Lulworth Castle, Wareham, Dorset BH20 5QS. Telephone: 0845 450 1054. Website: www.lulworth.com. Large one-manual organ by Richard Seede, 1785; restored William Drake, 1986–9. The console is 'reversed' in front of the case.

Macclesfield, Cheshire: Adlington Hall, near Macclesfield SK10 4LF. Telephone: 01625 827595. Website: www.adlingtonhall.com. Anonymous two-manual organ, c.1690; restored Mander, 1959. The largest surviving seventeenth-century organ in Britain; includes the original reed stops.

Manchester: Bridgewater Hall, Lower Mosley Street, Manchester M2 3WS. Telephone: 0161 907 9000. Website: www.bridgewater-hall.co.uk. Large four-manual organ by Marcussen, 1996.

Manchester: Heaton Hall, Heaton Park, off Middleton Road, North Manchester, M25 2SW. Telephone: 0161 773 1231. Website: www.manchestergalleries.org. Large two-manual organ originally built by Samuel Green, 1790.

Manchester: Royal Northern College of Music, 124 Oxford Road, Manchester M13 9RD. Telephone: 0161 907 5200. Website: www.rncm.ac.uk. Large three-manual classical organ by Hradetzky, 1973. The Watson Collection includes a barrel organ.

Manchester: Town Hall, Albert Square, Manchester M60 2LA. Telephone: 0871 1222 8223. Website: www.manchester2002-uk.com. Five-manual organ originally built by Cavaillé-Coll, 1877, 1893.

Moorlinch, Somerset: Blessed Virgin Mary Church. Chamber organ by James Davis, c.1790. Includes original nag's head swell.

Mundford, Norfolk: St Leonard's Church. Small three-manual organ by Harrison & Harrison, 1912, in a case by Comper.

Newcastle upon Tyne: Cathedral. Four-manual organ by Nicholson, 1981, incorporating a case by Renatus Harris, 1676.

Northleach, Gloucestershire: Keith Harding's World of Mechanical Music, The Oak House, High Street, Northleach GL54 3ET. Telephone: 01451 860181. Website: www.mechanicalmusic.co.uk. Includes a barrel organ and other mechanical 'organs'.

Norwich, Norfolk: Cathedral. Large four-manual organ by Hill, Norman & Beard, 1940–1, 1968–70. The second largest cathedral organ in Britain.

Norwich, Norfolk: Holy Trinity Church, Heigham. Organ by Frederick Rothwell, 1921, with the stops in between the manuals, a particular trait of Rothwell organs, now very rare.

Norwich, Norfolk: The Old Meeting House, Colegate. Case and some pipes from a seventeenth-century organ, possibly by Robert Dallam.

Norwich, Norfolk: St George's Church, Colegate. Organ by George Pike England, 1802.

Norwich, Norfolk: St Peter Mancroft Church. Large three-manual Werkprinzip organ by Peter Collins, 1983.

Nottingham: Albert Hall, North Circus Street, off Derby Road, Nottingham NG1

5AA. Telephone: 0115 950 0411. Website: www.albert-hall-nottingham.com. Large four-manual organ by J. J. Binns, 1909, restored Harrison & Harrison, 1992/3.

Nottingham: St Mary's Parish Church. Two-manual classical organ, complete with Brustwerk folding doors, by Marcussen of Denmark, 1973. A smaller instrument, by the same builder, can be found in St Mary's, Clifton, Nottingham.

Nottingham: Wollaton Hall Natural History Museum, Telephone: 0115 915 5555. Two-manual organ in the Great Hall gallery dating originally from *c*.1650; restored by N.P. Mander in 1980.

Old Bilton, Warwickshire: St Mark. Case by Dallam, 1636, originally made for St John's College, Cambridge.

Old Radnor, Powys: St Stephen's Church. Anonymous sixteenth-century case, *c*.1540, reputedly the oldest in Britain.

Oundle, Northamptonshire: Oundle School. Three-manual Werkprinzip organ by Frobenius of Copenhagen, 1984.

Oxford: Christ Church Cathedral. Four-manual classical organ by Rieger, 1979, but partly housed in Bernard Smith's original 1680s case.

Oxford: Holywell Music Room, Holywell Street. Two-manual organ (without pedals), originally built by John Donaldson of Newcastle upon Tyne, 1790; restored Mander, 1985.

Oxford: Jesus College. Modern two-manual organ in an eighteenth-century English style by William Drake, 1994.

Oxford: Magdalen College. Two-manual organ by Mander, 1985/6. The Great organ is in the 'Chair' position, in a stone case on the chapel screen.

Oxford: New College. Large three-manual Werkprinzip organ by Grant, Degens & Bradbeer, 1969.

Oxford: Queen's College. Two-manual organ by Frobenius of Copenhagen, 1965. One of the first Werkprinzip organs in Britain.

Oxford: St Mary the Virgin. Three-manual organ by Metzler of Zürich, 1987.

Oxford: Town Hall, 109–113 St Aldates, Oxford OX1 1DS. Telephone: 01865 252195. Website: www.oxford.gov.uk. Four-manual organ by 'Father' Willis, 1897.

Paisley, Renfrewshire: Abbey. Four-manual organ by J. W. Walker, 1968, with pipework from the organ by Cavaillé-Coll, 1872.

Peterborough, Cambridgeshire: Cathedral. Large four-manual organ by Hill, originally built 1894 and little altered since; restored Harrison & Harrison, 1980/1.

Portsea, Hampshire: St Mary's Church. Large three-manual organ by J. W. Walker, 1889.

Preston, Lancashire: St George the Martyr's Church. Three-manual 'Father' Willis organ, 1865, largely unaltered.

Reading: Town Hall. Four-manual organ by 'Father' Willis, 1864, 1882; restored Harrison & Harrison, 1999.

Ripon, North Yorkshire: Minster. Four-manual organ by Harrison & Harrison, 1913, 1926, 1963/4, 1972, 1987, incorporating pipework by Lewis & Renn and a case by Gilbert Scott of 1878.

Romsey, Hampshire: Abbey. Large three-manual organ by J. W. Walker, 1858, 1888; restored and enlarged by Mander, 1982, and Walker, 1975, 1992, 1995.

Rotherham, South Yorkshire: Parish Church. Present organ incorporates parts of the original Snetzler instrument of 1777.

Rugby, Warwickshire: Brownsover Church. Part of the case is possibly from Robert Dallam's 1636 organ for St John's College, Cambridge, now also at Old Bilton. The upper part of the case is probably from Thomas Thamar's *c*.1662 Chair case for St John's College, Cambridge.

St Albans, Hertfordshire: Abbey. Large four-manual organ by Harrison & Harrison, 1961/2, with minor alterations in 1973 and 1989, and extensive enlargement in 2009.

St Albans, Hertfordshire: St Albans Organ Museum, 320 Camp Road, St Albans AL1

Douai Abbey, Upper Woolhampton, near Reading, Berkshire. Three-manual organ by Kenneth Tickell. Note the grilles concealing the Swell manual.

5PE. Telephone: 01727 873896. Website: www.stalbansorgantheatre.org.uk. Includes several fairground organs and two cinema organs, one a Wurlitzer built originally for the Granada, Edmonton, in 1933, the other built by Spurden Rutt for the Regal, Highams Park.

St Andrews, Fife: University Church. Four-manual organ by Hradetzky, 1973/4.

St Bees, Cumbria: St Mary and St Bega. Three-manual organ by 'Father' Willis, 1899, enlarged Harrison & Harrison, 1906, 1931, 1949.

Salford, Manchester: St Paul's Church. Two-manual organ by Samuel Green, 1788, largely unaltered; originally built for St Thomas's, Ardwick, and restored by Hill, Norman & Beard, 1969.

Salford, Manchester: St Philip's Church. Two-manual organ by Renn & Boston, 1829, largely unaltered; restored Mander, 1963.

Salisbury, Wiltshire: Cathedral. Four-manual organ by 'Father' Willis, 1876; modified slightly by Willis, 1934, and restored 1969 and 1978. Reputed to be his best cathedral organ.

Salisbury, Wiltshire: St Thomas's Church. Organ originally built by Samuel Green, 1792, for the cathedral. Much original pipework appears to survive.

Saltaire, West Yorkshire: Museum of Victorian Reed Organs and Harmoniums, Victoria Hall, Victoria Road, Saltaire, Shipley BD18 3JS. Telephone (after 6.00 p.m.): 01274 585601 or 0976 535980. Website: www.harmoniumnet.nl/museum-Saltaire-ENG.html. The only museum of its kind in Europe; includes a piano-harmonium.

Selby, North Yorkshire: Abbey. Large four-manual organ originally built by Hill, 1909; restored and enlarged 1950, 1975.

Sherborne, Dorset: Abbey. Large three-manual organ originally built by Gray & Davison, 1856; restored 1986/7, 1991; virtually new organ by Kenneth Tickell, 2005, including a new 'nave' department. Includes a nineteenth-century example of a Chair case.

Shrewsbury, Shropshire: St Mary the Virgin's Church. Four-manual organ largely by Gray & Davison, with case and some pipes from the organ by Harris & Byfield of 1729.

Stanford-on-Avon, Northamptonshire: St Nicholas's Church. Early organ case (1630s) on west gallery. The instrument is thought to have been the Chair section from the organ originally in Magdalen College, Oxford, the remainder of which is now in Tewkesbury Abbey.

Staunton Harold, Leicestershire: Private Chapel. Contains a small organ reputed to be the work of Bernard Smith; restored Mander, 1955.

Teigngrace, Devon: St Peter and St Paul's Church. Two-manual organ originally built by James Davis, 1781.

Tewkesbury, Gloucestershire: Abbey. Choir organ incorporates the case and front pipes from an organ probably built by Robert Dallam for Magdalen College, Oxford, in 1631. Often called the 'Milton' organ because it was played by John Milton when the organ was moved to Hampton Court for Oliver Cromwell's benefit. The case and some pipework have been incorporated into a new four-manual organ (also incorporating parts of the 1948 Walker organ) by Kenneth Jones Associates, 1997. Four-manual North Transept organ originally built by Michell & Thynne for the Inventions Exhibition of 1885. Their *magnum opus*, the organ is one of the high points of the British romantic organ movement. Restored by Bishop & Son, 1980/1.

Thaxted, Essex: Parish Church. Large three-manual organ by Henry Lincoln, 1821, largely untouched. Small organ contains material by George Pike England.

Thornage, Norfolk: All Saints Church. Chamber organ by Thomas Elliot, 1812.

Thursford, Norfolk: The Thursford Collection, Thursford Green, Thursford, Fakenham NR21 0AS. Telephone: 01328 878477. Website: www.thursford.com. Contains several fairground or dance organs and a Wurlitzer theatre organ originally built for the Paramount Theatre, Leeds.

Truro, Cornwall: Cathedral. Almost untouched four-manual 'Father' Willis organ of 1888; restored Willis, 1963, Mander, 1991.

Twickenham, Middlesex: All Hallows' Church. Organ originally built by Renatus Harris, 1695.

Usk, Monmouthshire: St Mary's Church. Three-manual organ by Gray & Davison, 1860, originally built for Llandaff Cathedral; restored Nicholson, 2005; includes an en chamade trumpet stop.

Wakefield, West Yorkshire: Cathedral. Five-manual organ by Compton, 1951/2, partly built using the extension principle; restored and rebuilt by Wood, 1985.

Warrington, Cheshire: Parr Hall. Telephone: 01925 442345. Website: www.pyramidparrhall.co.uk. Organ originally built by Cavaillé-Coll, 1870.

Wells, Somerset: Cathedral. Four-manual Harrison & Harrison organ, 1909/10, 1973, based on an 1857 'Father' Willis instrument.

West Bromwich, West Midlands: Town Hall. Largely untouched three-manual organ by Forster & Andrews, 1878, 1888. Includes original Barker Lever action.

Whaplode St Catherine, Lincolnshire: Rutland Cottage Music Museum, Millgate, Whaplode St Catherine, Spalding PE12 6SF. Telephone: 01406 540379. Includes church, chamber, barrel and reed organs, as well as an 'orgapian', a combined organ and piano for accompanying films.

Whissonsett, Norfolk: St Mary the Virgin's Church. Chamber organ by Richard Nicholson, *c*.1850; restored Richard Bower, 2005.

Wigan, Lancashire: St Peter's Church, Hindley. Three-manual organ by Schulze, 1873. Organ currently unusable.

Winchester, Hampshire: Cathedral. Large four-manual organ by Willis/Harrison & Harrison based on 'Father' Willis's organ for the Great Exhibition of 1851. Includes a 'nave' section, added in 1988.

Winchester, Hampshire: Winchester College Chapel. Large three-manual organ by Mander, 1984, in case by W. D. Caroe, 1908.

Windsor, Berkshire: St George's Chapel, Windsor Castle. Large four-manual organ by Harrison & Harrison, 1965/6.

Wolverhampton: St John's Church. Case and some pipes by Renatus Harris, 1697, from Christ Church Cathedral, Dublin, said to be originally part of the instrument built for the 'battle of organs' between Harris and 'Father' Smith at the Temple Church, London.

Woodstock, Oxfordshire: Blenheim Palace, Woodstock OX7 1PX. Telephone: 08700 602080. Website: www.blenheimpalace.com. Three-manual organ by 'Father' Willis, 1891, in the Long Library. The instrument can be played automatically as well as by an organist.

Worcester: Cathedral. Four-manual Quire organ by Kenneth Tickell, 2008; two Nave organs are also planned.

Wymondham, Norfolk: Abbey. Large three-manual organ by James Davis, 1793. Rebuilt 1954, 1973. One-manual chamber organ also by Davis, 1810.

York: Minster. Large four-manual organ first built in 1829 by Elliot & Hill and originally the largest organ in Britain. Rebuilt at various times by J. W. Walker, Harrison & Harrison and Principal Pipe Organs. The original Gothick case remains.

Uppingham School, Rutland. Organ by Rushworth & Dreaper. Three manuals and horizontal trumpet stop.

5
Further reading

Andersen, P-G. *Organ Building and Design*. Allen & Unwin, 1969.

Archbold, L. and Peterson, W.J. *French Organ Music: from the Revolution to Franck and Widor*. University of Rochester Press, 1999.

Arnold, C.R. *Organ Literature: A Comprehensive Survey* (two volumes). Third edition. Scarecrow Press, 1995.

Barnes, A. and Renshaw, M. *The Life and Work of John Snetzler*. Scolar Press, 1994.

Bicknell, S. *The History of the English Organ*. Second edition. Cambridge University Press, 1999.

Boeringer, J. *Organa Britannica: Organs in Great Britain 1660-1860* (three volumes). Associated University Press, 1983/6.

Bush, D. and Kassell, R. *The Organ: an Encyclopedia*. Routledge, 2006.

Clutton, C. and Niland, A. *The British Organ*. Second edition. Eyre Methuen, 1982.

Donahue, T. *Modern Classical Organ: A Guide to its Physical and Musical Structure*. McFarland, 1991.

Douglass, F. *Cavaillé-Coll and the French Romantic Tradition*. New edition. Yale University Press, 1999.

Douglass, F. *The Language of the Classical French Organ: A Musical Tradition before 1800*. Revised edition. Yale University Press, 1995.

Downes, R. *Baroque Tricks: Adventures with the Organ Builders*. Positif Press, 1999.

Edson, J.S. *Organ Preludes: An Index to Compositions on Hymn Tunes, Chorales, Plainsong Melodies, Gregorian Tunes and Carols* (two volumes). Scarecrow Press, 1970.

Elvin, L. *Bishop and Son, Organ Builders: the Story of J.C. Bishop and His Successors*. Published by the author, 1984.

Elvin, L. *Family Enterprise: the Story of some North Country Organ Builders*. Published by the author, 1986.

Elvin, L. *Forster and Andrews, Organ Builders, 1843-1956: A Chapter in English Organ Building*. Published by the author, 1968.

Elvin, L. *Forster and Andrews, their Barrel, Chamber and Small Church Organs*. Published by the author, 1976.

Elvin, L. *The Harrison Story*. Published by the author, 1977.

Elvin, L. *Organ Blowing: Its History and Development*. Published by the author, 1971.

Elvin, L. *Pipes and Actions: Some Organ Builders in the Midlands and Beyond*. Published by the author, 1995.

Freeman, A. *Father Smith: Otherwise Bernard Schmidt, Being an Account of a Seventeenth Century Organ Maker*. Positif Press, 1977.

Goodrich, W. *The Organ in France* (1917) New version published. Kessinger Publishing, 2009.

Grace, H. *French Organ Music, Past and Present*. Bibliobazaar, 2009.

Hardwick, P. *British Organ Music of the 20th Century*. Scarecrow Press, 2002.

Harmon, T.F. *The Registration of J.S. Bach's Organ Works: a Study of German Organ-Building and Registration Practices of the late Baroque Era*. Organ Literature Foundation, 1978.

Henderson, J. *A Directory of Composers for Organ*. Third edition. Published by the author, 2005.

Henshaw, W.B. *A Bibliography of Organ Music*. Second edition. Bardon Enterprises, 2002.

Hiles, J. *Catechism of the Organ*. Packebusch, Germany: Bardon Enterprises, 2005.

Hill, A.G. *The Organ-Cases and Organs of the Middle Ages and Renaissance* (reprint of 1883-91 edition). Library Reprints, 2001.

Hirst, B. *Just a Box of Whistles: Secrets of the Art of Organ Pipe Making*. Front Rank Books, 2001.

Hopkins, E.J. and Rimbault, E.F. *The Organ: Its History and Construction* (reprint of 1877 edition). Travis & Emery, 2009. Includes specifications of many famous nineteenth-century organs.

Hughes, B. *The Schulze Dynasty: Organ Builders 1688-1880*. Musical Opinion Ltd, 2006.

Hurford, P. *Making Music on the Organ*. New edition. Oxford University Press, 1990. A comprehensive study of organ-playing technique and interpretation.

Landon, J.W. *Behold the Mighty Wurlitzer: History of the Theatre Pipe Organ*. Greenwood, 1983.

Langwill, L.G. and Boston, N. (1970) *Church and Chamber Barrel Organs*. Second edition. Published by author, 1970.

Longhurst, J. *Magnum Opus: The Building Of The Schoenstein Organ At The Conference Centre Of The Church Of Jesus Christ Of Latter-Day Saints*. Deseret Book Company, 2009.

The five-manual organ console and case of St Paul's Cathedral, London, built by N. P. Mander, 1977, based on the 'Father' Willis organ of 1872. The cases are from the original Bernard Smith organ of 1697, designed by Sir Christopher Wren. It includes a 'nave' section.

Lukas, V. *A Guide to Organ Music.* Fifth edition. Amadeus Press, 2003.

Neal, R. *Organ Registrations and Techniques.* Sceptre Publication, 1982.

Norman, H. and Norman, J. *The Organ Today.* New edition. David and Charles, 1980.

Norman, J. *The Organs of Britain: an Appreciation and Gazetteer.* David and Charles, 1984.

Norman, J. *The Box of Whistles: Organ Case Design.* Azure, 2007.

Norman, J. and Berrow, J. *Sounds Good: A Guide to Church Organs, for Incumbents, Churchwardens and PCCs.* Church House Publishing, 2002.

Ord-Hume, A.W.J.G. *Barrel Organ: the Story of the Mechanical Organ and its Repair.* Allen and Unwin, 1987.

Ord-Hume, A.W.J.G. *Harmonium: the History of the Reed Organ and its Makers.* David and Charles, 1986.

Owen, B. *The Registration of Baroque Organ Music.* Indiana University Press, 1999.

Pacey, R. *The Organs of Oxford: an Illustrated Guide to the Organs of the University and City of Oxford.* Second edition. Positif Press, 1997.

Perrot, J. *The Organ, from its Invention in the Hellenistic Period to the End of the Thirteenth Century.* Oxford University Press, 1971.

Plumley, N.M. *The Organs of the City of London: from the Restoration to the Present.* Positif Press, 1996.

Rimbault, E. *New History of the Organ.* University Press of the Pacific, 2005. Originally published 1877.

Routh, F. *Early English Organ Music from the Middle Ages to 1837.* Barrie and Jenkins, 1973.

Rowntree, J.P. and Brennan, J.F. (1975-1993) *The Classical Organ in Britain* (three volumes). Positif Press. Specifications, line drawings and photographs of 'classical' organs built 1945 to 1990.

Rowntree, J.P. *Organs in Britain, 1990-1995.* Published by the author, 1996.

Sayer, M. *Samuel Renn: English Organ Builder.* Phillimore, 1974.

Shannon, J. *Understanding the Pipe Organ.* McFarland & Co., 2009.

Azuchi Seminario Hall, Japan. New organ by N. P. Mander.

Stauffer, G.B. *J.S. Bach as Organist: His Instruments, Music, and Performance Practices.* Batsford, 1986.

Sumner, W.L. *The Organ: Its Evolution, Principles of Construction and Use.* Fourth edition. MacDonald and Jane's, 1973.

Sutton, J. *A Short Account of Organs Built in England from the Reign of King Charles II to the Present Time.* Positif Press, 1979.

Thistlethwaite, N.J. *The Making of the Victorian Organ.* Second edition. Cambridge University Press, 1992.

Thistlethwaite, N.J. *The Organs of Cambridge: an Illustrated Guide to the Organs of the University and City of Cambridge.* Positif Press, 1993.

Thistlethwaite, N.J. and Webber, G. *The Cambridge Companion to the Organ.* Cambridge University Press, 1999.

Whitney, C. *All the Stops.* Public Affairs, 2004.

Wickens, D. *Aspects of English Organ Pipe Scaling.* Positif Press, 2004.

Wickens, D.C. *The Instruments of Samuel Green.* Scarecrow Press, 1987.

Williams, C. *The Story of the Organ* (1903). New version published. Kessinger Publishing, 2009.

Williams, P.F. *The European Organ, 1450-1850.* Batsford, 1966. A detailed and comprehensive study.

Williams, P.F. *The King of Instruments: How Churches Came to Have Organs.* SPCK, 1993.

Williams, P.F. *A New History of the Organ: from the Greeks to the Present Day.* Faber, 1998.

Williams, P.F. *The Organ in Western Culture, 750-1250.* Second edition. Cambridge University Press, 2005.

Williams, P.F. (1985-1999) *The Organ Music of J.S. Bach* (three volumes). New edition. Cambridge University Press, 2003. The definitive study of Bach's organ music.

Williams, P.F. and Owen, B. *The Organ* (The Grove Musical Instrument Series). Macmillan, 1988. Includes glossaries of stop names and organ-building terms and a list of major organ builders past and present.

Wills, A. *Organ.* Second edition. Kahn & Averill, 1998.

Wilson, M.I. *Organ Cases of Western Europe.* C. Hurst, 1979.

Wilson, M.I. *The Chamber Organ in Britain, 1600-1830.* Second edition. Ashgate, 2001.

Wyatt, G. *At the Mighty Organ.* Oxford Illustrated Press, 1974.

6
Useful addresses

In most areas of the United Kingdom there is an association or club for those interested in the organ and its music. Details can normally be obtained through the Incorporated Association of Organists (see below). There are also specialist societies for devotees of the fairground organ, the cinema organ and the barrel organ. It is possible to join an email list where enthusiasts and experts discuss issues relating to all aspects of the organ and organ music. See, for example, ORGUE-L@cdmnet.org (website: http://cdmnet.org/cgi-bin/mailman/listinfo/orgue-l) and the online *Encyclopedia of Organ Stops* (www.organstops.org/). Below is a select list of special-interest groups. Their websites (detailed) link to many other such sites. Local public library services should also be able to provide useful addresses.

Association of Independent Organ Advisors (AIOA), College of St Barnabas, Lingfield, Surrey, RH7 6NJ. Telephone: 01473 219102. Website: www.aioa.org.uk.

British Institute of Organ Studies (BIOS), Ashcroft, 10 Ridgegate Close, Reigate, Surrey, RH2 0HT. Telephone: 01737 241355. Website: www.bios.org.uk.

British Institute of Organ Studies Journal, Positif Press, 130 Southfield Road, Oxford OX4 1PA. Telephone: 01865 243220. Fax 01865 243272. Website: www.bios.org.uk, www.positifpress.com/journals.htm.

Choir and Organ, Rhinegold Publishing, 239-241 Shaftesbury Avenue, London, WC2H 8TF. Telephone: 020 7333 1705. Website: www.rhinegold.co.uk/magazines/choir_and_organ Emai: choirandorgan@rhinegold.co.uk.

Incorporated Association of Organists (IAO), 17 Woodland Road, Northfield, Birmingham B31 2HU; website: www.iao.org.uk. (The IAO publishes *Organists' Review*, available from Allegro Music, 43 The Hop Pocket Craft Centre, New House Farm, Bishops Frome, Worcs, WR6 5BT. Telephone: 01885 490375. Website: www.iao.org.uk/organists-review/index.asp.
Allegro Music is now the membership agency for the IAO and queries should be addressed to them.)

Institute of British Organ Building, 13 Ryefields, Thurston, Bury St Edmunds, Suffolk IP31 3TD. Telephone: 01359 233433. Website: www.ibo.co.uk.

London Organ Concerts Guide, LOCG, Causeway House, The Causeway, Boxford, CO10 5JR. Website: www.londonorgan.co.uk.

The Organ, Telephone: 01424 715167. Website: www.theorganmag.com Email: editor@theorganmag.com.

Organ Club, 92 The Hawthorns, Charvil, Reading, RG10 9TS. Telephone: 020 7278 0801. Website: www.organclub.org.

Organ Historical Society, PO Box 26811, Richmond, Virginia, 232261. Email: www.organsociety.org.

Organs and Organists Online, Website: http://organsandorganistsonline.co.uk.

Royal College of Organists, PO Box 56357, London, SE16 7XL. Telephone: 05600 767208. Website: www.rco.org.uk.

7
Discography

The following list of recordings aims to provide a representative sample of organ music on compact disc, though not all the recordings listed are necessarily currently available for purchase. The first sequence of recordings is arranged according to composer. These discs usually contain music by one or at most two composers. The second sequence is arranged according to artist. The final section lists anthologies of organ music played by two or more different organists. Discs in the second and third listings contain pieces by many different composers. After the composer, artist and other details, the name of the recording company is given, followed by the disc number.

Many recording companies have their own website giving details of current (and back) stock lists and forthcoming recordings. A number of organisations also aim to provide a broader listing of recordings of the organ. These include *Gothenburg Organ Academy* (website: http://goart.gu.se/gioa/); *The Organ* (website: www.theorganmag.com).

COMPOSERS

Alain, Jehan. *Complete Organ Works* – Marie-Claire Alain: Erato 8572-80214-2. *Organ Works* (2 volumes) – Eric Lebrun: Naxos 8.553632/3. *Complete Organ Works: volume 2.* Marie-Claire Alain. Erato 8573-85773-2

Andriessen, Hendrik. *Complete Organ Works* – Albert de Klerk, St Josephkerk, Haarlem: Lindenberg LBCD 31/34 (4 CDs).

Arne, Thomas. *The Six Organ Concertos* – Roger Bevan Williams: Chandos CHAN 8604.

Bach, Carl Philipp Emanuel. *Organ Works* – Peter van Dijk: Lindenberg LBCD 35.

Bach, Johann Sebastian. *Organ Works* – Marie-Claire Alain: Erato 4509-96358-2 (14 CDs). Bram Beekman on historic Dutch organs (9 parts): Lindenberg LBCD 17/18; 26/27; 36/37; 41/42; 45/46; 48/49; 52/53; 56/57; 62/63. Christopher Herrick on various Metzler organs in Switzerland: Hyperion CDA 67213/4; 66791/2; 66813; 67215; 67139; 67211/2; 66756; 66455; 67071/2; 66434; 66390; 67263. Werner Jacob: EMI 7243 573878 2 8 (16 CDs; 4 volumes). Piet Kee, St Bavokerk Haarlem, the Martini Church, Groningen: Chandos CHAN 0506, 0510, 0527. *Organ Works* – Ton Koopman: Deutsche Grammophon 410 999-2; 427 801-2; 431 119-2; 447 277-2; 447 292-2; Teldec CD 88-99. *Organ Works* – Simon Preston: Deutsche Grammophon 469 420-2 (14 CDs). *Organ Works* – Wolfgang Rübsam: Naxos 8.505024; 8.505034; 8.550184; 8.550651; 8.550652; 8.550653; 8.550703; 8.550704; 8.550790; 8.550901; 8.550927; 8.550929; 8.550930; 8.553031; 8.553032; 8.553033; 8.553134; 8.553135; 8.553150; 8.553629; 8.553859; 8.553936; 8.554444. *Organ Works* – Helmut Walcha: Deutsche Grammophon 453 064-2; 457 704-2. *Various Organ Works* – Piet Kee, St Laurens' Church, Alkmaar, Holland: Chandos CHAN 0501. *Organ Mass* – Peter Dyke, St Albans Abbey: Lammas LAMM 092D. *Complete Orgelbüchlein* – Alexander Fisiesky, Steinkirchen: Lammas LAMM 099D. *Organ Works in Romantic Arrangements* – Wolfgang Baumgratz, Sauer Organ of Berlin Cathedral: MDG 320 0761-2. *Pro Cembalo Pleno: Bach on the Pedal Harpsichord* – Douglas Amrine: Priory PRCD 523.

Baumann, Max. *Organ Works* (2 volumes): MDG 315 1084-2; 315 1085-2.

Best, William Thomas. *Organ Works* – Christopher Nickol, St Patrick's Cathedral, Dublin: Priory PRCD 681.

Bovet, Guy. *Organ Works* – Guy Bovet: MDG 320 0675-2.

Brahms, Johannes. *Complete Organ Works* – Rudolf Innig: MDG 317 0137-2.

Bridge, Frank. *Organ Works* – Christopher Nickol, Caird Hall, Dundee: Priory PRCD 537.

Bruhns, Nicolaus. *Various Organ Works* – Piet Kee, Roskilde Cathedral, Denmark: Chandos CHAN 0539.

Buxtehude, Dietrich. *Complete Organ Works* (7 volumes) – Harald Vogel, mainly on Schnitger organs: MDG 314 0268-70-2; MDG 314 0424-7-2. *Organ Music* – Marie-Claire Alain: Erato 0630-12979-2 (2 CDs; 2 volumes). Volker Ellenberger: Naxos 8.554543; 8.555775. *Various Organ Works* – Piet Kee, Roskilde Cathedral, Denmark: Chandos CHAN 0539; and St Laurens' Church, Alkmaar, Holland: Chandos CHAN 0501; CHAN 0514.

Clérambault, Nicolas. *Livre d'Orgue* – Jean Boyer: Virgin 5 61777 2.

Cochereau, Pierre. *Improvisation: the Illusionist's Art* – David Briggs, Truro Cathedral: Priory PRCD 428.

Couperin, François. *Organ Masses* – Jean-Patrice Brosse: Virgin 5 61298 2 (2 CDs). *Organ Works* – Jan Willem Jansen: Virgin 5 61775 2.

Daquin, Louis-Claude. *Twelve Noëls* – Christopher Herrick: Hyperion CDA 66816.

Darke, Harold. *Organ Works* – Jonathan Rennert, St Michael's, Cornhill, London: Priory PRCD 374.

De Grigny, Nicolas. *Premier Livre d'Orgue* – Marie-Claire Alain: Erato 3984-27443-2.

Dupré, Marcel. *Complete Organ Music* (3 volumes): MDG 316 0951-3-2. *Complete Organ Works* – Jeremy Filsell: Guild GMCD 7156; 7157; 7159; 7162; 7164; 7173; 7180; 7183; 7188; 7193; 7198; 7203. *Organ Music* – John Scott, St Paul's Cathedral: Hyperion CDA 66205; 67047. *Works for Organ* (12 volumes): Naxos 8.553862; 8.553918; 8.553922; 8.553919; 8.554026; 8.554210; 8.554211; 8.553920; 8.554378; 8.553921; 8.554379; 8.554209.

Duruflé, Maurice. *Organ Music* – John Scott, St Paul's Cathedral: Hyperion CDA 66368. *Sacred Choral and Organ Works* (2 volumes) – Eric Lebrun: Naxos 8.553196-7.

Eben, Petr. *Organ Music* (3 volumes) – Holger Schiager: Hyperion CDA 67194-6.

Eberlin, Johann Ernst. *Organ Works* – Florian Pajitsch: MDG 320 0767-2.

Finzi, Gerald. *Organ Music* – Robert Gower, Hereford Cathedral: Priory PRCD 591.

Franck, César. *Complete Organ Works* – Bram Beekman, Perpignan Cathedral: Lindenberg LBCD 91-3. *Great Organ Works* – Marie-Claire Alain: Erato 0630-12706-2 (2 CDs). *Various Organ Works* – Piet Kee, Royal Concertgebouw: Chandos CHAN 8891; Eric Lebrun, Cavaillé-Coll organ of Saint-Antoine des Quinze-Vingts, Paris: Naxos 8.554697.

Frescobaldi, Girolamo. *Fiori Musicali; Il Secondo Libro de Toccate* – Ton Koopman: Erato 4509-96544-2.

Gibbons, Orlando. *Complete Organ Works* – Robert Woolley, Ploujean, France: Chandos CHAN 0559. *Choral and Organ Music* – Laurence Cummings: Naxos 8.553130.

Gigout, Eugène. *Complete Organ Works* (5 volumes) – Gerard Brooks: Priory PRCD 761-5.

Guilmant, Alexandre. *Organ Works* – Henk van Putten: Lindenberg LBCD 60.

Hakim, Naji. *Organ Music* – Naji Hakim and Marie-Bernadette Duforcet, Sacré-Coeur, Paris: Priory PRCD 465.

Handel, George Frideric. *The Organ Concertos* – Simon Preston: Deutsche Grammophon 469 358-2 (3 CDs). Paul Nicholson, St Laurence Whitchurch: Hyperion CDA 67291/2 (2 CDs). Herbert Tachezi: Teldec 4509-91188-2 (2 CDs). *Organ Concertos Opus 4/2, 4-5; Opus 7/1; No 13*: Naxos 8.550069. *Organ Concertos Opus 4/1-2, 4-5, 13* – Jane Watts: Priory CHIX 699. *Organ Works in Romantic Arrangements* – Wolfgang Baumgratz, Sauer organ of Berlin Cathedral: MDG 320 0761-2.

Harwood, Basil. *Complete Organ Works* (4 volumes) – Adrian Partington: Priory PRCD 683-4, 781, 792.

Haydn, Joseph. *Organ Concertos* – Ton Koopman: Erato 0630-17070-2.

Hertel, Johann Wilhelm. *Organ Sonatas* – Martin Rost: MDG 320 1103-2.

Hindemith, Paul. *Sonatas 1-3* – Piet Kee, St Bavokerk, Haarlem, Holland: Chandos CHAN 9097.

Hollins, Alfred. *Organ Music* – David Liddle, Hull City Hall: Priory PRCD 398.

Howells, Herbert. *Organ Works* (3 volumes) – Graham Barber, Stephen Cleobury, Adrian Partington: Priory PRCD 480, 524, 547.

Jackson, Francis. *Sounds of Francis Jackson* – Simon Nieminski, St Mary's Cathedral, Edinburgh: Lammas LAMM 127D.

Karg-Elert, Sigfrid. *Organ Works* – Jaap Kroonenburg, Grote Kerk, Maassluis: Lindenberg LBCD 54.

Krebs, Johann Ludwig. *Complete Organ Works* – John Kitchen: Priory PRCD 734-9. *Organ Music* – Franz Ramil: MDG 614 0971-2 (2 CDs). *Organ Works* – John Kitchen: MDG 331 0384-2.

Labor, Josef. *Organ Works* – Ian Coleman, St Ignatius, Stamford Hill, London: Priory PRCD 688.

Leighton, Kenneth. *Complete Organ Works* – Dennis Townhill: Priory PRCD 326 ABC (3 CDs).

Lemmens, Jacques-Niclas. *Organ Music* – Ben van Oosten: MDG 316 0975-2.

Liddle, David. *Organ Music*: David Liddle, St Ignatius Loyola, New York: Guild. GMCD 7130.

Liszt, Franz. *Liszt at St Paul's Cathedral* – John Scott: Guild GMCD 7128. *Organ Works* – Nicolas Kynaston: Guild GMCD 7210.

Lloyd Webber, William. *Organ Works* – Jane Watts, Salisbury Cathedral: Priory PRCD 616.

Mahler, Gustav. *Symphony no. 5* – transcribed and played by David Briggs, Gloucester Cathedral: Priory PRCD 649.

Martini, G. Battista. *Organ Music* – Ennio Cominetti: MDG 606 0998-2.

Mendelssohn, Felix. *Organ Works* – Jan Jansen, Utrecht Cathedral: Lindenberg LBCD 43/4. John Scott, St Paul's Cathedral: Hyperion CDD 22029 (2 CDs). *Organ Sonatas, opus 65* – Stephen Tharp: Naxos 8.553583. Rudolf Innig: MDG 317 0487-2 (2 CDs).

Merkel, Gustav. *Complete Organ Sonatas* (4 volumes) – Adrian Partington: Priory PRCD 501, 522, 548-9.

Messiaen, Olivier. *Complete Organ Works* – Olivier Messiaen: EMI 0777 767400 2 7 (4 CDs). Olivier Latry: Deutsche Grammophon 471 480-2 (6 CDs). Rudolf Innig (6 volumes): MDG 317 0009-2; 0346-2; 0621-2; 0053-2; 0622-2; 0622-2 (2 CDs). Willem Tanke: Lindenberg LBCD 77/84 (8 CDs). *Le Livre du Saint Sacrement* – Anne Page, Norwich Cathedral: Guild GMCD 7228/9 (2 CDs). *La Nativité du Seigneur* – Malcolm Archer, Coventry Cathedral. Kevin Mayhew: 1490019. Louise Marsh, Wakefield Cathedral: OxRecs OXCD-86.

Mozart, Wolfgang Amadeus. *Complete Church Sonatas for Organ and Orchestra* – Geneviève Soly: Chandos CHAN 8745. *Organ Music* – Christiaan Ingelse, St-Janskerk, Gouda: Lindenberg LBCD 23.

Pachelbel, Johann. *Music for Organ* – Werner Jacob: Virgin 7 59197 2.

Parry, Hubert. *Complete Organ Works* – James Lancelot: Priory PRCD 682 AB (2 CDs).

Poulenc, François. *Organ Concerto* – Gillian Weir: Virgin 5 61979 2.

Reger, Max. *Complete Organ Works* (12 volumes) – Rosalinde Haas, Albiez-Organ in Frankfurt-Niderrad: MDG 315-0350-61-2. *Organ Masterworks* – Franz Hauk: Guild GMCD 7192. *Various Organ Works* – Piet Kee, St Bavokerk, Haarlem, Holland: Chandos CHAN 9097. *Complete Bach Organ Arrangements* – Rosalinde Haas: MDG 315 0484-2 (2 CDs).

Reubke, Julius. *Organ Works* – Jeremy Filsell: Guild GMCD 7137.

Rheinberger, Josef. *Complete Organ Works* (6 volumes) – Rudolf Innig: MDG 317 0891-6-2.

Ritter, August Gottfried. *Organ Sonatas* – Ursula Philippi: MDG 320 0866-2.

Saint-Saëns, Camille. *Organ Symphony*: Deutsche Grammophon 435 854-2; 419 617-2; 439 014-2 (different performers).

Scheidemann, Heinrich. *Works for Organ* (3 volumes) – Julia Brown, Karin Nelson, Peter van Dijk: Naxos 8.554202; 8.554203; 8.554548.

Schumann, Camillo. *Organ Sonatas* – Reinhard Kluth: MDG 606 0173-2 (2 CDs).

Schumann, Robert. *Complete Organ Works* – Rudolf Innig: MDG 317 0619-2.

Stanford, Charles. *Complete Organ Sonatas* – Desmond Hunter: Priory PRCD 445 AB (2 CDs).

Stanley, John. *Organ Voluntaries* – Richard Marlow, Trinity College, Cambridge: Chandos CHAN 0639.

Sweelinck, Jan Pieterszoon. *Organ Works* – James Christie: Naxos 8.550904. *Various Organ Works* – Piet Kee, St Laurens' Church, Alkmaar, Holland: Chandos CHAN 0514.

Tallis, Thomas. *Organ Works* – Robert Woolley, Ploujean, France: Chandos CHAN 0588.

Telemann, Georg Philipp. *Organ Works* – Wolfgang Baumgratz: MDG 320 0078-2.

Tomkins, Thomas. *Complete Keyboard Music* – Bernhard Klapprott: MDG 607 0563-2; 0704-6-2. *Choral and Organ Music* – Laurence Cummings: Naxos 8.553794.

Tournemire, Charles. *Organ Music* – Marie-Bernadette Duforcet, Sacré-Coeur, Paris: Priory PRCD 328.

Vaughan Williams, Ralph. *Organ Works* – Christopher Nickol, Caird Hall, Dundee: Priory PRCD 537.

Vierne, Louis. *Complete Organ Symphonies* – Ben van Oosten: MDG 316 0732-2 (4 CDs). *Organ Symphonies* – James Lancelot, Iain Simcock: Priory PRCD 236; 446; 425; 590. *Organ Works* – Ben van Oosten: MDG 316 0847-2 (2 CDs).

Walton, William. *Organ Music* – Robert Gower, Hereford Cathedral: Priory PRCD 591.

Weckmann, Matthias. *Organ Works* (2 volumes) – Wolfgang Zerer: Naxos 8.553849-50.

Weitz, Guy. *Organ Works* – Paul Derrett, Hereford Cathedral: Priory PRCD 410.

Whitlock, Percy. *Complete Organ Works* – Graham Barber: Priory PRCD 489; 525; 542.

Widor, Charles Marie. *Complete Organ Works* (7 volumes) – Ben van Oosten: MMDG 316 0401-6-2; 0519-2. *Organ Symphony no. 5* – David Hill, Westminster Cathedral: Hyperion CDA 66181. Simon Preston: Deutsche Grammophon 413 438-2.

Wills, Arthur. *Organ Works* – Jeremy Filsell: Guild GMCD 7225.

ARTISTS

Alain, Marie-Claire. *The Bach Family: Organ Works*: Erato 0630-17073-2. *A Celebration:* Erato 0630-15343-2 (5 CDs). *Famous Organ Music:* Erato 2292-45976-2. *Great Toccatas:* Erato 4509-94812-2. *Noëls:* Erato 0630-17823-2. *Organ Encores:* Erato 4509-92888-2.

Archer, Malcolm. *Organ Favourites* – Hereford Cathedral: Kevin Mayhew 1490002. *The Organ of the Colston Hall, Bristol:* Priory PRCD 305. *The Organ of Lancaster Town Hall:* Priory PRCD 400. *Sounds Magnificent* – Wells Cathedral: Lammas LAMM 112.

Austin, Michael. *Organ Classics* – Birmingham Town Hall: Chandos CHAN 6518.

Ball, Ian. *Sounds Symphonic: French Masterworks for Organ* – Gloucester Cathedral: Lammas LAMM 126D.

Barber, Graham. *The Organ of Coventry Cathedral:* Priory PRCD 373. *The Organ of Ripon Cathedral:* Priory PRCD 769. *The Organ of St Bartholomew's Church, Armley:* Priory PRCD 269. *The Organ of St Johannis, Osnabrück, Germany:* Priory PRCD 297. *The Organ of Salisbury Cathedral:* Priory PRCD 314. *The Organ of the Jacobijnerkerk, Leeuwarden, Holland:* Priory PRCD 520. *The Organ of Villingen Minster, Germany:* Priory PRCD 391.

Baumgratz, Wolfgang. *Organ Landscape Holstein* (2 volumes): MDG 319 0962-2; 1025-2. *Organ Landscape Schleswig / Sonderjlland:* MDG 319 0913-2.

Benedetti, Luigi. *The Organ of Milan Cathedral:* Priory PRCD 427.

Bertero, Roberto. *The Organ of St Eustache, Paris, France:* Priory PRCD 690.

Blatchly, Mark. *The Organ of Lancing College Chapel:* Priory PRCD 521.

Bleazard, David. *The Organ of St John the Baptist, Kensington:* Priory PRCD 601.

Bolt, Klaas. *Freu dich sehr:* Lindenberg LBCD 97. *Inspired by Arp Schnitger:* Lindenberg LBCD 94. *St-Maartenskerk, Zaltbommel:* Lindenberg LBCD 16.

Bowman, Calvin. *Great Australasian Organs Series, 4, 5:* Priory PRCD 661-2.

Brayne, Christopher. *The Organ of Bristol Cathedral:* Priory PRCD 380.

Briggs, David. *Great Organ Transcriptions:* Kevin Mayhew 1490008. *Improvisations* – St Paul's and Hereford Cathedrals: Kevin Mayhew 1490023. *The Organ of Gloucester Cathedral:* Priory PRCD 685; 568. *The Organ of St George's Hall, Liverpool:* Priory PRCD 284. *The Organ of St John's Church, Upper Norwood:* Priory PRCD 680.

Brooks, Gerard. *The Organ of St François de Sale, Lyon, France:* Priory PRCD 667. *The Organ of St Ouen, Rouen, France:* Priory PRCD 558. *The Organ of St Pierre, Douai, France:* Priory PRCD 637.

Charlston, Terence. *The Glory of Baroque* – Douai Abbey: Kevin Mayhew 1490022.

Chorosinski, Andrzej. *Virtuoso Organ Music:* MDG 320 0818-2.

Cleobury, Stephen. *British Organ Music from King's College, Cambridge:* Priory PRCD 005. *The Organ of King's College, Cambridge:* Priory PRCD 185.

Crowley, Robert. *Sounds Contemporary* – All Saints, Margaret Street: Lammas LAMM 103.

Culp, James. *In a Monastery Garden*: Guild GMCD 7212.

Curly, Carlo. *Organ Favourites*: Decca. 458 364-2.

De Gier, Gerrit. *St-Stevenskerk, Nijmegen*: Lindenberg LBCD 50.

Duforcet, Marie-Bernadette. *The Organ of Notre-Dame-Des-Champs, Paris, France*: Priory PRCD 422.

Eisenberg, Matthias. *The Organ of St Georgenkirche, Rötha, Germany*: Priory PRCD 411.

Farr, Stephen. *The Organ of Odense Cathedral, Denmark*: Priory PRCD 458.

Filsell, Jeremy. *The Oxford Book of Wedding Music* – Lancing College Chapel: Guild GMCD 7101. *Three English Romantics* – St Luke's, Chelsea: Kevin Mayhew 1490021. *Virtuoso Organ Works*: Guild GMCD 7144.

Fiseisky, Alexander. *Bach and German Romantic Organ Music*: Lammas LAMM 108. *Russian Organ Music*: Lammas LAMM 101.

Goode, David. *French Showpieces from King's College, Cambridge*: Kevin Mayhew 1490018.

Gough, Rupert. *The Organ of Wells Cathedral*: Priory PRCD 595.

Green, Gareth. *English Organ Music*: Naxos 8.550582.

Hakim, Naji. *Canticum* – *French Organ Music*: EMI 7243 572272 2 3. *The Organ of the Sacré-Coeur, Paris*: Priory PRCD 369.

Hancock, Judith. *The Organ of St Thomas Church, Fifth Avenue, New York, USA*: Priory PRCD 599.

Herrick, Christopher. *Organ Dreams*: Hyperion CDA 67060; 67146. *Organ Fireworks*: Hyperion CDA 66121; 66258; 66457; 66605; 66676; 66778; 66917; 66978; 67228.

Heywood, Thomas. *Who Needs an Orchestra?* Melbourne Town Hall: Pro Organo CD 7141.

Hunt, Donald. *English Organ Music 2*: Naxos 8.550773.

Hurford, Peter. *Romantic Organ Works*: Decca 466 742-2 (2 CDs). *Organ Favourites*: Decca 452 166-2.

Jackson, Nicholas. *The Organ of Segovia Cathedral, Spain*: Priory PRCD 423.

Jakob, Hans-Otto. *The Organ of Frankfurt Imperial Cathedral, Germany*: Priory PRCD 615.

Janca, Jan. *Danzig Organ Landscape*: MDG 319 1115-2.

John, Keith. *The Organ of the Hallgrímskirkja, Reykjavík, Iceland*: Priory PRCD 532. *The Organ of the Kallio Church, Helsinki, Finland*: Priory PRCD 638.

Jongepier, Jan. *Gereformeerde Kerk 'De Rank' Zuidhorn*: Lindenberg LBCD 24.

Judd, Roger. *The Organ of St Laurenskerk, Rotterdam*: Priory PRCD 689.

Kee, Piet. *At the Concertgebouw*: Chandos CHAN 9188.

King, Peter. *The Organ of Bath Abbey*: Priory PRCD 335; PRC 618.

Kitchen, John. *The Organ of the Reid Concert Hall, Edinburgh*: Priory PRCD 627.

Kiviniemi, Kalevi. *Christmas Organ*: Finlandia 3984-22015-2. *Finnish Organ Music*: Finlandia 3984-27891-2. *French Organ Music*: Finlandia 0630-18399-2; 4509-98035-2. *Organ Encores*: Finlandia 4509-98034-2. *Renaissance and Early Baroque Organ Music*: Finlandia 4509-98036-2. *The Wedding Organ Album*: Finlandia 3984-22016-2.

Kroonenburg, Jaap. *Groote Kerk Maassluis*: Lindenberg LBCD 10; 87.

Kurpershoek, Liesbeth. *The Organ of St Mary's Anglican Cathedral, Johannesburg*: Priory PRCD 610.

Kynaston, Nicolas. *The Klais Organ of Megaron, the Athens Concert Hall, Athens, Greece*: Priory PRCD 780.

Lancelot, James. *The Organ of Durham Cathedral*: Priory PRCD 228; 346. *The Organ of Emmanuel Church, Chestertown, Maryland, USA*: Priory PRCD 640.

Lawrence, Douglas. *Bamboo Organ of Los Piñas, Manila, Philippines*: available in the UK from The Divine Art Record Company, MD 3136 (telephone: 0191 456 1837 website: www.divine-art.com).

Le Grice, Ian. *The Organ of the Temple Church, London*: Priory PRCD 569.

Lemckert, Johann. *St-Laurenskerk, Rotterdam*: Lindenberg LBCD 14.

Liddle, David. *Organ of St Ignatius Loyola, New York*: Guild GMCD 7149.

Lindley, Simon. *French Organ Music*: Naxos 8.550581. *Town Hall Classics* – Leeds Town Hall: OxRecs OXCD-71.

DISCOGRAPHY

Lucas, Adrian. *The Organ of Portsmouth Cathedral*: Priory PRCD 561.
Lucas, Andrew. *Organ Showpieces from St Paul's Cathedral*: Naxos 8.550955.
Marshall, Wayne. *Get Organised: Transcriptions for Organ*: Virgin 5 61703 2. *Symphonie*: Virgin 5 45320 2.
Matthews, Charles. *The Organ of La Madeleine, Paris, France*: Priory PRCD 772.
Murray, Thomas. *The Organ of Yale University, USA*: Priory PRCD 338.
Nethsingha, Andrew. *The Organ of Truro Cathedral*: Priory PRCD 695.
Nickol, Christopher. *The Organ of Dunblane Cathedral*: Priory PRCD 606.
Norris, Hilary. *The Organ of Ashridge Chapel, Berkhamsted, Hertfordshire*: Priory PRCD 741.
Olesen, Kristian. *The Organ of Roskilde Cathedral, Denmark*: Priory PRCD 444.
Orlinski, Heinz Bernhard. *Silesian Organ Landscape*: MDG 319 0135-2.
Pagitsch, Florian. *Carinthian Organ Landscape*: MDG 319 0766-2. *Salzburg Organ Landscape*: MDG 319 0990-2.
Pardee, Katharine. *Blending Voices: Organ Music from Belgium*: Pro Organo CD 7140.
Parkins, Robert. *Early Iberian Organ Music*: Naxos 8.550705.
Parnell, Andrew. *Penitence and Praise* – St Albans Abbey: Kevin Mayhew 1490010.
Partington, Adrian. *The Organ of Reading Town Hall*: Priory PRCD 687.
Payne, Joseph. *Early English Organ Music* (2 volumes): Naxos 8.550718-19. *German Organ Music* (2 volumes): Naxos 8.550964/5.
Philippi, Ursula. *Transylvanian Organ Landscape*: MDG 319 0414-2 (2 CDs).
Poulter, David. *Fanfare for Organ* – Coventry Cathedral: Kevin Mayhew 1480027. *Toccatas from Coventry Cathedral*: Lammas LAMM 097D.
Preston, Simon. *The World of the Organ*: Decca 430 091-2.
Quinn, Ian. *Tsar of Instruments [Russian Organ Music]*: Chandos CHAN 10043.
Rabin, Yuval. *Organ Music from Israel*: MDG 606 1072-2.
Rennert, Jonathan. *The Organ of St Michael's Church, Cornhill, London*: Priory PRCD 375.
Reymeier, Konstantin. *The Organ of St Jacobi, Hamburg*: Priory PRCD 607.
Roloff, Elisabeth. *Jerusalem Organ Landscape*: MDG 319 0538-2.
Rost, Martin. *Mecklenburg Organ Landscape*: MDG 319 0430-2 (2 CDs).
Roth, Daniel. *The Cavaillé-Coll organ of St Sulpice, Paris, France*: Priory PRCD 767.
Sayer, Roger. *The Organ of the Hallgrímskirkja, Reykjavík, Iceland*: Priory PRCD 495.
Schönheit, Michael. *Thüringian Organ Landscape*: MDG 319 0552-2 (3 CDs).
Scott, John. *The Organ of St Giles' Cathedral, Edinburgh*: Priory PRCD 485. *The Organ of St Ignatius Loyola, New York, USA*: Priory PRCD 643. *The Organ of St Paul's Cathedral, London*: Priory PRCD 401.
Sharpe, Robert. *Sounds Majestic* – Lichfield Cathedral: Lammas LAMM 114.
Stewart, Gordon. *Voluntaries and Interludes* – Huddersfield Town Hall: OxRecs OXCD-72.
Thomas, James. *Organ Masterworks* – Chichester Cathedral: Kevin Mayhew 1490016.
Tracey, Ian. *Bombarde!* – *French Organ Classics* – Liverpool Cathedral: Chandos CHAN 9716. *Music for Organ and Orchestra by Guilmant, Widor, Poulenc* – Liverpool Cathedral: Chandos CHAN 9271; 9785.
Wagler, Dietrich. *The Organ of Freiburg Dom, Germany*: Priory PRCD 332.
Walsh, Colin. *The Organ of Lincoln Cathedral*: Priory PRCD 281; 379; 477. *The Organs of Salisbury and Lincoln Cathedrals*: Priory PRCD 648.
Watts, Jane. *Great Australasian Organs Series, 1, 2, 3, 6, 7*: Priory PRCD 515-7; 775-6. *The Organ of Rochester Cathedral*: Priory PRCD 389. *The Organ of St John's Smith Square, London*: Priory PRCD 491. *The Organ of the Kelvingrove Art Gallery, Glasgow*: Priory PRCD 414. *The Organ of the Ulster Hall, Belfast*: Priory PRCD 377. *The Organ of Westminster Abbey, London*: Priory PRCD 237.
Weir, Gillian. *Organ Master Series* (3 volumes): Priory PRCD 751-3.
Whiteley, John Scott. *The Organ of St Ouen, Rouen, France*: Priory PRCD 619. *The Organ of Sheffield City Hall*: Priory PRCD 674. *The Organ of York Minster*: Priory PRCD 487.
Wills, Arthur. *Music for Organ and Brass* – Ely Cathedral: Helios CDH55003.
Wilson, George. *Dunblane Cathedral*: Lindenberg LBCD 22.

Woolley, Robert. *Organ Music of Purcell, Blow, Locke and Gibbons* — Guimiliau Church, Brittany, France: Chandos CHAN 0553.

Wright, Peter. *The Organ of Southwark Cathedral, London*: Priory PRCD 406.

ANTHOLOGIES

Arp Schnitger in Groningen. Lindenberg LBCD 12; 15.

Baroque Organs in Mecklenburg. MDG 520 1061-2.

Celebration of the Rieger Organ of UNISA, South Africa. Priory PRCD 609.

Great Toccatas for Organ. EMI 7243 575356 2 5 (2 CDs).

LBCD Organ Collection. 4 volumes: Lindenberg LBCD 91; 94; 97; OC4.

Organ Concertos by Wesley, Handel, Stanley, Arne. Gerard Brooks/Noel Tredinnick: Priory PRCD 439.

Organ Extravaganza. Malcolm Archer, David Briggs and Noel Rawsthorne: Kevin Mayhew 1490078.

Organ Music from the Island of Ireland. John Dexter — St Patrick's, Dublin. Francis Jackson — Down Cathedral.

Organ of Durham Cathedral. Priory PRCD 746.

Organa Antiqua Bohemica. Lindenberg LBCD 71/74; 75/6.

Organbuilders Verschueren. Lindenberg LBCD 28/29.

Organbuilders Witte. Lindenberg LBCD 67/70.

Organs of Cambridge. 4 volumes: OxRecs OXCD-59-60.

Organs of Eton College. 2 volumes: OxRecs OXCD-65/6.

Organs of Oxford. 2 volumes: OxRecs OXCD-41/2.

Pipes of Splendour. Francis Jackson — York Minster. Michael Austin — old organ of Birmingham Town Hall: Chandos CHAN 6602.

Romantic Organs in Mecklenburg. MDG 520 1062-2.

Southwell Splendour. Paul Hale and Philip Rushforth — Nicholson organ of Southwell Minster: OxRecs OXCD-80.

1000 Years of Organs in Mecklenburg. MDG 54611.

12 Organs of Edinburgh. Priory PRCD 700 AB (2 CDs).

Urakami Cathedral, Nagasaki, Japan. New organ by N. P. Mander.

Index

INDEX